JOURNEYS

Reader's Notebook
Volume 2

Grade 3

Houghton Mifflin Harcourt

Printed in the U.S.A.

ISBN 978-0-544-59264-3

26 27 28 29 30   0304   26 25 24 23 22

4500846250   B C D E F G

Contents

Contents

Words with *air*, *ear*, *are*

**Write a word from the box to complete each sentence.
Then read the complete sentence.**

airfare	hear	wear
airline	pear	year
dairy	share	
prepare	tear	

1. The _____ has ten airplanes.

2. Gently _____ the paper into two pieces.

3. The teacher will _____ the lesson for the day.

4. Did you _____ the bell ring?

5. You must pay the _____ before you can ride
   on the plane.

6. Milk and cheese are in the _____ food
   group.

7. You and I were born in the same _____.

8. It's cold outside, so you'll need to _____
   your coat.

9. This is a juicy _____!

10. It's kind to _____ your toys.

Name _____   Date _____

Lesson 16
READER'S NOTEBOOK

Judy Moody Saves
the World!
Grammar:
What Are Adjectives and Articles?

Adjectives That Tell What Kind

Adjectives are words that describe, or tell about, nouns. Some adjectives tell what kind.

We went for a <u>long</u> walk. (What kind of walk?)

An adjective usually comes before the noun it describes.

Thinking Question
Which word tells what kind?

Write the adjective that tells about the underlined noun.

1. Our class started a recycling <u>project</u>. _____

2. Mr. Thomas put several big <u>bins</u> in the room.
_____

3. The blue <u>bin</u> was for paper. _____

4. Jason added a stack of old <u>newspapers</u>.
_____

5. Lee Ann brought wrapping <u>paper</u>. _____

6. Melissa used the colorful <u>paper</u> for a collage.
_____

7. We added our cereal <u>boxes</u> to the bin. _____

8. Our small <u>class</u> collected a lot of paper.
_____

9. We took the bins to a green <u>truck</u>. _____

10. The workers wore thick <u>gloves</u>. _____

Adjectives That Tell How Many

An **adjective** is a word that describes, or tells about, a noun. Some adjectives tell how many. An adjective that tells how many comes before the noun it describes.

She saw <u>three</u> birds in a nest. (How many birds?)

Thinking Question
Which word tells how many?

Write the adjective that tells about the underlined noun.

1. There are two <u>paths</u> along the river. _____

2. My dad hikes to the river with four <u>friends</u>.
   _____

3. They bring five <u>bags</u> to collect trash. _____

4. My dad picks up many <u>cans</u>. _____

5. Soon two <u>bags</u> are filled with trash. _____

6. Then they see several <u>cans</u> in the shallow river.
   _____

7. Three <u>men</u> have boots and wade into the water.
   _____

8. They use a net and pull seventeen <u>cans</u> out of the river.
   _____

9. A few more <u>pieces</u> of trash are under the bench.
   _____

10. Their walk home is about one <u>mile</u>. _____

Name _____ Date _____

Lesson 16
READER'S NOTEBOOK

Judy Moody Saves the World!
Spelling:
Vowel + /r/ Sounds in *air* and *fear*

Spelling Word Sort

Write each Basic Word under the correct heading.

Vowel + /r/ Sound in *air* spelled *air*	Vowel + /r/ Sound in *fear* spelled *ear*
_____	_____
_____	_____
_____	_____
_____	_____

Vowel + /r/ Sound in *air* spelled *ear*	Vowel + /r/ Sound in *air* spelled *are*
_____	_____
_____	_____
_____	_____

Basic
1. air
2. wear
3. chair
4. stairs
5. bare
6. bear
7. hair
8. care
9. pear
10. pair
11. share
12. near
13. ear
14. beard

Review
buy
year

Challenge
earring
compare

Review Add one Review Word to your Word Sort.

Which Review Word cannot be added to the Word Sort?

_____

Challenge: Add the Challenge Words to your Word Sort.

Focus Trait: Purpose
Introducing the Topic and Opinion

The purpose of a persuasive letter is to try to make someone believe something or take an action. Good writers state their opinion clearly and convince readers it is correct by giving specific reasons. For example, Monique does not like the school lunch menu because it includes too much junk food. She wants to convince the school board to change the menu so it includes more healthful foods, like fruits and vegetables. She might offer reasons, such as healthful foods help kids think better and have stronger bodies.

Read each writer's opinion and think about the writer's purpose and goal. Then read the reasons that could support the opinion. Underline the strongest, most convincing reasons.

1. We should help rescued dogs and cats. I want to convince people to adopt rescued animals.

   REASONS

   A. Pets are good.

   B. Adopting a rescued pet saves a life.

   C. Rescued pets have a lot of love to give owners.

   D. Some rescued pets are injured or sick.

2. We should clean up our local park. I want to convince my classmates to volunteer to help clean up the park.

   REASONS

   A. Kids are getting hurt on broken glass and metal litter.

   B. A lot of people use the park.

   C. We can be proud of the place where we play.

   D. Litter makes the park look bad.

Cumulative Review

Write a word from the box to complete each sentence in the story.
Then read the story.

careful	energy	wear
center	shirt	worry
dirty	turned	
disappeared	stairs	

"I want to _____ my new clothes," said Julia. She went up
                    1

the _____ to her room and put them on.
            2

Julia went back downstairs. She _____ the doorknob to
                                            3

go outside.

"Julia," said Mom, "don't get your new clothes _____."
                                                        4

"Don't _____, Mom. I'll be _____!"
            5   6

Julia _____ into the backyard. She used a lot of
            7

_____ playing outside. As she came back in, she saw a big
    8

spot in the _____ of her new _____. "Oh, no!"
                    9   10

she gasped. "I should have listened to Mom!"

Name _____ Date _____

Lesson 16
READER'S NOTEBOOK

Judy Moody Saves
the World!
Independent Reading

Reader's Guide

Judy Moody Saves the World!

Judy Moody's Class Presentation

"Judy Moody will come up to the front of the class and talk about what she has learned about the environment," said Mr. Todd.

Read pages 18–20. Use the information on these pages to help Judy tell the class how she got the idea to save the world.

_____

_____

_____

Read pages 21–22. Use these pages to help Judy tell the class about the Crazy Strips contest.

_____

_____

_____

Read pages 24–27. Use these pages to help Judy tell the class about her work the next morning. Then tell how her family felt about her plan.

_____

_____

_____

Read pages 28–29. Use these pages to help Judy tell about her next plan.

_____

_____

_____

Read pages 31–32. Help Judy tell how her family responded to this plan.

_____

_____

_____

Read pages 35–36. Help Judy tell the class how she decided to save trees and energy.

_____

_____

_____

Name _____ Date _____

Lesson 16
READER'S NOTEBOOK

Judy Moody Saves
the World!
Grammar:
What Are Adjectives and Articles?

This, That and Articles

- The adjectives *this* and *that* tell "which one."
- The words *a*, *an*, and *the* are adjectives called **articles.**
- Use *a* before nouns that begin with a consonant sound. Use *an* before nouns that begin with a vowel sound.

Underline the adjective that tells *which one*. Write the noun the adjective describes.

1. My friends and I helped clean this park. _____

2. We put the trash we collected in that can. _____

3. This playground could use a good cleaning. _____

Choose the article in parentheses to go with the underlined word. Write the article.

4. I have (a, an) <u>can</u> to recycle. _____

5. You should recycle (the, an) <u>paper</u>. _____

6. There is (a, an) <u>empty</u> bin. _____

7. (The, An) <u>bin</u> is not full yet. _____

Word Towers

Read each clue. Write the Basic Word that matches each clue.

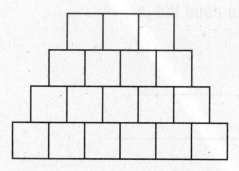

Clues

1. A body part you use to hear
2. Two of something
3. Hair on a man's chin

4. Fills the open space around you
5. A large, strong animal
6. Split something with a friend
7. Steps

Challenge Use Basic, Review, and Challenge Words to complete the Word Tower.

Clues

8. Pay money for something
9. Feel love and concern for someone
10. Furniture you can sit on
11. Steps
12. Tell how two things are alike

Spelling Words

Basic
1. air
2. wear
3. chair
4. stairs
5. bare
6. bear
7. hair
8. care
9. pear
10. pair
11. share
12. near
13. ear
14. beard

Review
buy
year

Challenge
earring
compare

Name _____ Date _____

Lesson 16
READER'S NOTEBOOK

Judy Moody Saves the World!
Vocabulary Strategies:
Context Clues

Context Clues

Write the meaning of the underlined word as it is used in each sentence. Circle the words that help you know the meaning of the underlined word.

1. One weekend each fall, our family goes on a <u>yearly</u> campout.

_____

2. When it gets dark, we gather <u>kindling</u> to start a campfire.

_____

3. Last year, our tent was <u>leaky</u>. Rain dripped in while we were sleeping.

_____

4. Our new tent is made from <u>recycled</u> bottles.

_____

5. This year, we forgot to put our <u>garbage</u> in the trash can with a lid.

_____

6. A raccoon <u>gobbled</u> up the food we threw away.

_____

7. My brother and I <u>quarreled</u> with loud voices over who was supposed to put the lid on the trash can.

_____

8. Pop got us to stop fighting when he <u>suggested</u> that we all go fishing.

_____

9. We got the <u>necessary</u> gear to catch fish and headed to the pond.

_____

10. We were sad to see the <u>pollution</u> in the pond.

_____

Name _____   Date _____

More Plural Nouns

- Form the **plural of a noun** that ends with a consonant and *y* by changing the *y* to *i* and adding *-es*.
- Identify nouns that change their spelling to form their plurals.

    The <u>families</u> enjoyed watching the <u>geese</u>.

Write the plural form of each singular noun in parentheses.

1. two beautiful (butterfly) _____

2. six new (hobby) _____

3. two intelligent (woman) _____

4. many falling (leaf) _____

5. a crowd of (child) _____

Write *singular* or *plural* for each underlined noun.

6. A <u>man</u> gathered bottles. _____

7. The <u>geese</u> flew over the recycling area. _____

8. Many <u>families</u> recycle their own garbage. _____

9. One <u>city</u> saves money by reusing paper. _____

10. <u>Mice</u> will eat garbage if it isn't cleaned up. _____

Name _____ Date _____

Lesson 16
READER'S NOTEBOOK

**Judy Moody Saves
the World!**

Spelling:
Vowel + /r/ Sounds in *air* and *fear*

Proofreading for Spelling

Read the following journal entry. Find and circle the misspelled words.

May 8

    Today I went camping in a park nere my home. Before I left, I took cair as I decided what to where. I put on a jacket because the aer was crisp. I put a cap over my haire. I wore a pare of hiking boots, too.

    I got to the campsite and set up my tent. I sat in my camp chare and started to eat a juicy paire. All of a sudden I saw a big, brown bair. He was looking at my food, but I did not want to shear. I ended my camping trip right then and there!

Spelling Words

Basic
1. air
2. wear
3. chair
4. stairs
5. bare
6. bear
7. hair
8. care
9. pear
10. pair
11. share
12. near
13. ear
14. beard

Review
buy
year

Challenge
earring
compare

Write the misspelled words correctly on the lines below.

1. _____   6. _____

2. _____   7. _____

3. _____   8. _____

4. _____   9. _____

5. _____   10. _____

Connect to Writing

Short Sentences	Longer, Smoother Sentence
Our class watched a video about recycling. The video about recycling was interesting.	Our class watched an interesting video about recycling.
There was a talking can in the video. The talking can was green.	There was a green talking can in the video.

Combine two short sentences by moving an adjective to make one longer sentence. Write the new sentence on the line.

1. The video was about a recycling center. The recycling center was big.

_____

2. Many people work in the recycling center. It is noisy in the recycling center.

_____

3. One worker wore a hat. The hat was huge.

_____

4. The wind blew paper into the air. The paper was yellow.

_____

5. The workers take a bus home. The bus is new.

_____

14

Name _____ Date _____

Lesson 17
READER'S NOTEBOOK

The Albertosaurus
Mystery
Phonics:
Words with /j/ and /s/

Words with /j/ and /s/

Read each sentence. Choose the missing word from the box. Write the word. Then reread the complete sentence.

season	decide	squirt
jelly	scale	jumping
force	edge	engine

1. Which _____ of the year is your favorite?

2. Close the door with _____ .

3. I would love to drive a fire _____ !

4. Place the apples on the _____ .

5. Felice likes to put _____ on her toast.

6. The _____ on these scissors is too dull to

    cut cardboard.

7. "Did you _____ who is the winner?" the girl

    asked.

8. If you _____ me with water, I'll have to

    change my clothes.

9. We saw grasshoppers _____ into the

    bushes.

Adding *-er*, *-ier*, or *More*

- Add *-er* to most **adjectives** that have one syllable.
- For adjectives that have two syllables and end in *-y*, such as *happy*, replace the *y* with *i* and then add *-er*.
- Add *more* before adjectives that have two or more syllables.

    The pottery is <u>larger</u> than the arrowheads.

    The arrowheads were <u>shinier</u> than the pottery.

    The Native American exhibit is <u>more modern</u> than the dinosaur exhibit.

Thinking Questions
Does the adjective have more than one syllable? Does it end in -y?

Choose the correct form of the adjective in parentheses. Write it on the line.

1. The (younger, more young) of the two students found an arrowhead made of stone. _____

2. The arrowhead was in a location (deeper, more deep) than the clay pot. _____

3. One of the bones was (tinier, more tiny) than the arrowhead. _____

4. It was (difficulter, more difficult) to unearth the arrowheads than the bones. _____

5. The circle of stones was (interestinger, more interesting) than the bones they found. _____

Name _____ Date _____

Lesson 17
READER'S NOTEBOOK

The Albertosaurus
Mystery
Grammar:
Adjectives That Compare

One-Syllable Adjectives That Compare

- Add *-er* to most **adjectives** that have one syllable.
- For adjectives with one syllable that end in a single vowel followed by a consonant, double the last consonant and then add *-er*.

  Are the Badlands <u>hotter</u> than a desert?

Thinking Questions
Does the adjective have only one syllable? Does it end in a single vowel followed by a consonant?

Write the correct form of the adjective that compares two nouns.

1. fresh _____

2. green _____

3. fat _____

4. sad _____

5. hard _____

6. cool _____

7. thin _____

8. tight _____

9. soft _____

10. ripe _____

Name _____ Date _____

Lesson 17
READER'S NOTEBOOK

The Albertosaurus
Mystery
Spelling:
Words with /j/ and /s/

Spelling Words with /j/ and /s/

1. Write the Basic Words that use the letter *j* to spell the sound /j/.

_____ , _____ ,

_____

2. Write the Basic Words that use the letter *g* to spell the sound /j/.

_____ , _____ ,

_____ , _____ ,

_____

3. Write the Basic Word that uses the letter *s* to spell the sound /s/.

_____

4. Write the Basic Words that use the letter *c* to spell the sound /s/.

_____ , _____ ,

_____ , _____ ,

_____ , _____

Challenge

1. gigantic Circle the letter in *gigantic* that makes one of this week's spelling sounds.

2. excited Circle the letter in *excited* that makes one of this week's spelling sounds.

Spelling Words
Basic
1. age
2. space
3. change
4. jawbone
5. jacket
6. giant
7. pencil
8. circle
9. once
10. large
11. dance
12. jeans
13. bounce
14. huge
Review
nice
place
Challenge
excited
gigantic

Focus Trait: Elaboration
Interesting and Supporting Details

Good writers elaborate on their ideas with interesting details that support their opinions. Interesting details can make your writing seem more convincing.

Weak Details: I think computers are a waste of time.

Interesting Details: Computers can be a big help doing some tasks, but it's important to do more than just sit in front of a monitor all day. How about getting outside and playing with friends?

Which sentence is more interesting?

Read each sentence. Revise sentences so they include more interesting details.

1. Our cafeteria food is not very good.

   _____

   _____

   _____

2. I think school sports are great.

   _____

   _____

   _____

3. I think homework should be more fun.

   _____

   _____

   _____

Words with the VCCCV Pattern

Write a word from the box to complete each
sentence. Then read the complete sentence.

explore	partner	improve
instant	complaining	laundry
complicated	dolphin	athlete

1. I know that if I practice I will _____.

2. We made _____ oatmeal since we had no
time to cook breakfast.

3. Cara is a great _____ who swims and plays
soccer.

4. When we paired up, I chose Gloria as my

_____.

5. Tran is always _____ that it is too cold.

6. This puzzle is too _____ for young children.

7. When we were at the beach, we saw a

_____ in the sea.

8. Mom is teaching me to do my own _____.

9. I would like to travel and _____ the world.

Name _____ Date _____

Lesson 17
READER'S NOTEBOOK

The Albertosaurus
Mystery
Independent Reading

Reader's Guide

The Albertosaurus Mystery:
Philip Currie's Hunt in the Badlands

Clues in the Attic

You are exploring an old attic and you find a large wooden chest. You read the name *Barnum Brown* scrolled across the back. The chest must belong to Barnum Brown! As you uncover each object inside the chest, help tell the story of Barnum Brown's discoveries.

First, you find a photograph of an old plow.

Read page 64. Use what you learn on this page and write why Barnum Brown kept this photo.

_____

_____

_____

You continue digging through the chest and find a photograph of T. rex bones.

Read page 65. Use information from this page to decide why this photograph was important to Barnum Brown.

_____

_____

_____

Name _____ Date _____

Lesson 17
READER'S NOTEBOOK

The Albertosaurus
Mystery
Independent Reading

Inside the wooden chest, you also find an old journal wrapped in cloth. You open to a page and begin reading Philip Currie's journal entries.

Read pages 69–70. What did Philip Currie write in his journal about his findings in the museum basement? What did he do as a result? Write as if you were Philip Currie.

_____

_____

_____

Read pages 71–72. Use this information to write in Philip Currie's journal about his main question.

_____

_____

_____

Read pages 73–75. Use this information to write in Currie's journal about Rodolfo Coria and what the two scientists concluded.

_____

_____

_____

Name _____ Date _____

Lesson 17
READER'S NOTEBOOK

The Albertosaurus
Mystery
Grammar:
Adjectives That Compare

Comparing More Than Two Nouns

- Add *-est* to most **adjectives** that have one syllable.
- For adjectives with two or more syllables, add the word *most* before the adjective.
- For adjectives with two syllables that end in *-y*, such as *happy*, replace the *y* with an *i* and then add *-est*.
- For adjectives that have one syllable and end in a single vowel followed by a consonant, first double the last consonant and then add *-est*.

  Which of the world's oceans is the deepest?

  She chose the most expensive book.

  Of the three jokes, Ben's is the funniest.

Thinking Questions
Does the adjective compare more than two nouns? Does it have more than one syllable? Does it end in -y?

Write the correct form of the adjective that compares more than two nouns.

1. happy _____

2. wonderful _____

3. fast _____

4. thin _____

5. sleepy _____

6. dangerous _____

Lesson 17
READER'S NOTEBOOK

The Albertosaurus
Mystery
Spelling:
Words with /j/ and /s/

Spelling Words with /j/ and /s/

1. Four of the words on the list are synonyms for *big*.
Write them on the lines. You may write Basic Words
and Challenge Words.

_____, _____,

_____, _____

2. Write three sentences about a dinosaur. Use
four of the spelling words. Don't use any synonyms
for *big*!

_____

_____

_____

_____

_____

_____

Spelling Words

Basic
1. age
2. space
3. change
4. jawbone
5. jacket
6. giant
7. pencil
8. circle
9. once
10. large
11. dance
12. jeans
13. bounce
14. huge

Review
nice
place

Challenge
excited
gigantic

Name _____ Date _____

Lesson 17
READER'S NOTEBOOK

The Albertosaurus Mystery
Vocabulary Strategies:
Suffix -ly

Suffix -*ly*

Circle the word in each sentence that has the suffix -*ly*.
On the line, write the meaning of the word.

1. The angry dog growled fiercely.

_____

2. The truck driver honked the horn loudly when the light
turned green.

_____

3. Maria won the race easily because she is the fastest
runner in our class.

_____

4. We watched hopefully as Sean tried to score the winning
goal.

_____

5. When he saw his birthday present, Jason laughed happily.

_____

6. The students read quietly in the library until the bell rang.

_____

7. Mom told Sara that she sang beautifully in the school play.

_____

8. We walked carefully across the shaky bridge.

_____

Writing Proper Nouns

- A **proper noun** names a particular person, pet, place, holiday, person's title, or book title.
- Always begin a proper noun with a capital letter.

  Aunt Liz took me to the Museum of Natural History.

Identify the proper nouns in each sentence. Then write each sentence correctly.

1. My favorite holiday is hanukkah, and it is in december.

   _____

2. That is one of mrs. hubbard's favorite movies.

   _____

Use proofreading marks to write each proper noun in this letter correctly.

Dear grandma,

   Last week our class at beacon school learned about cats. We looked

at a book called all kinds of cats. My friend tracy brought her cat to class.

Her cat's name is fuzzy. Her cat was a valentine's day present.

                              Love,
                              Amy

Proofreading for Spelling

Find the misspelled words and circle them.

A long, long time ago, a jiant ship flew through outer spase. It was the shape of a pensil, but it was gijantic. It flew in a sircle around the Earth. It flew around the Earth onse, then twice, then three times. In fact, it flew around the Earth a hundred times! What was it doing? What was it looking for? No one knows. Maybe the people on the ship wanted to chanje planets. Maybe they liked to bounse from world to world and never stop. Maybe their world was not larje enough for them. I have a different answer, though. I think thcy were looking for a place to buy geans. They just came here thousands of years too soon.

Spelling Words

1. age
2. space
3. change
4. jawbone
5. jacket
6. giant
7. pencil
8. circle
9. once
10. large
11. dance
12. jeans
13. bounce
14. huge

Review
nice
place

Challenge
excited
gigantic

Write the misspelled words correctly on the lines below.

1. _____   6. _____

2. _____   7. _____

3. _____   8. _____

4. _____   9. _____

5. _____   10. _____

Connect to Writing

Use adjectives to describe how people, places, or things are different. To compare two nouns, add *-er* to most adjectives. To compare more than two nouns, add *-est* to most adjectives.

Compare Two	Compare More Than Two
This bone is older than that one.	This is the oldest bone we have found.
It is hotter today than yesterday.	We went digging on the hottest day of the week.

Use the correct form of the adjective in parentheses. Write the sentence.

1. *Tyrannosaurus Rex* was (big) than *Albertosaurus*.

   _____

2. The (long) dinosaur measured more than 100 feet in length.

   _____

3. Sauropod eggs are (thick) than chicken eggs.

   _____

4. One of the (large) dinosaur eggs was found in China.

   _____

Words with /k/ and /kw/

Read each sentence. Choose the missing word from the box. Write the word. Then reread the complete sentence.

croaking	music	squeal
jacket	quiet	joke
squirrel	sock	tractor

1. Kim told a silly _____ that made us all giggle.

2. It is cold outside, so wear a warm _____.

3. After everyone went to bed, the house was very

_____.

4. My brother's band plays loud _____.

5. "Here is my shoe, but where is my _____?"
Ana asked.

6. We saw a _____ in a tree at the park.

7. Mr. Martin got a new _____ for his farm.

8. The scared little pig let out a loud _____.

9. You can hear frogs _____ down by the pond.

The Verb *be*

The verb *be* has different forms. Different subjects use these different forms. *Am*, *is*, and *are* show present tense. *Was* and *were* show past tense.

> Ms. Greene <u>was</u> our teacher last year.
> We <u>were</u> interested in her book on deserts.
> One large desert <u>is</u> in Africa.

Thinking Question
What is the subject, and do I want to show present tense or past tense?

Choose the correct verb in ( ), and write it on the line.

1. My science project (am, is) finished. _____

2. Ms. Burns (was, were) happy that I finished.

_____

3. Leaves (was, were) part of my project. _____

4. They (was, were) very colorful. _____

5. Mike's project (is, are) also finished. _____

6. Forest animals (is, are) in his project. _____

7. They (was, were) fun for him to draw. _____

8. We (am, are) proud of our projects. _____

9. The projects (is, are) on a table. _____

10. Our room (is, are) ready for Parent Night.

_____

Name _____ Date _____

Lesson 18
READER'S NOTEBOOK

A Tree Is Growing
Grammar:
Using the Verb *be* and
Helping Verbs

Helping Verbs

Helping verbs work with the main verb to help show time.
Singular and plural subjects use different forms.

Subject	Helping Verbs
Singular nouns Pronouns: he, she, it	is, was, has
Plural nouns Pronouns: you, we, they	are, have, were
Pronoun: I	am, was, have

The tree was growing taller.
It has grown many branches.

The two friends were talking quietly.
We have tried to count the leaves.
They are blowing in the wind.

I am going to stop counting.
I was excited about the falling leaves.

Thinking Questions
Is the subject of the sentence singular or plural? If it is a pronoun, what form of helping verb does it take?

Write the correct verb in ( ) to complete the sentence.

1. Those workers (is, are) planting trees in the park. _____

2. My brother (is, are) helping the workers. _____

3. He (has, have) asked me to come with him. _____

4. I (am, is) going to walk with them. _____

5. One tree's leaves (has, have) already turned brown. _____

6. Some squirrels (was, were) collecting acorns. _____

Spelling the /k/ and /kw/ Sounds

Write each Basic Word where it belongs in the chart.

<u>k</u>ite	tri<u>ck</u>
_____	_____
_____	_____
	_____

<u>c</u>amp	<u>qu</u>ack
_____	_____
_____	_____
_____	_____
_____	_____

Challenge: Add the Challenge Words to your Word Sort.

Spelling Words

Basic
1. shark
2. check
3. queen
4. circus
5. flake
6. crack
7. second
8. squeeze
9. quart
10. squeak
11. quick
12. coldest
13. Africa
14. Mexico

Review
black
thank

Challenge
correct
question

32

Focus Trait: Conventions

Exact Words

> Good writers of persuasive problem-and-solution paragraphs use exact words—nouns, adjectives, adverbs, and verbs—to express clearly what they want to say. Compare a sentence without exact words and a sentence with exact words.
>
> **Without Exact Words:** The dog chased the cat.
>
> **With Exact Words:** The large, playful golden retriever chased the tiny calico cat.

Rewrite each sentence, adding exact words to express the writer's thoughts more clearly. Make up your own specific details and exact words.

1. The piano fell.

_____

_____

2. The puppy tripped.

_____

3. The store manager told me to leave.

_____

4. From the window, you can see many things.

_____

5. The food was great.

_____

Name _____ Date _____

Lesson 18
READER'S NOTEBOOK

A Tree Is Growing
Phonics:
Cumulative Review

Cumulative Review

Write a word from the box to complete each sentence about one family's love for the zoo. Then read the complete sentence.

complain	kiss	quality
exchange	monkey	question
instead	pick	surprise

1. I have never heard anyone _____ about our local zoo.

2. It isn't a huge zoo, but its _____ is very good.

3. Our zookeepers have managed to _____ animals with zoos in faraway places.

4. My favorite animal is a _____ from India.

5. He likes to blow you a _____ when you visit his exhibit.

6. My little brother would _____ the zebra as his favorite animal.

7. It's probably no _____ that my sister likes the koalas best.

8. Our family would choose a visit to the zoo _____ of almost any other form of entertainment.

9. We all often ask the _____, "Can we go to the zoo this weekend?"

Reader's Guide

A Tree Is Growing

Label a Growing Tree

What did you learn about trees? Use the features in *A Tree Is Growing* to help you draw and label a growing tree.

Read pages 94–96. Draw and label three different leaves. Write a caption telling what leaves do for trees.

_____

_____

_____

Read pages 97–99. What is sap? What is special about some kinds of sap? Use the captions to find some of this information.

_____

_____

_____

35

Read pages 100–101. What are some important things about a tree's roots?

_____

_____

Read pages 102–105. What are some important things about a tree's bark?

_____

_____

Now draw a picture of your own growing tree. Use the information from the text and illustrations to label your tree's parts.

Using Verbs

Choose the correct verb in ( ), and write it on the line.

1. The pine tree (is, are) the tallest tree in the woods. _____

2. The lakes in our state (is, are) very pretty. _____

3. The Hudson River (is, am) the longest river in New York State.

   _____

4. Our trip to Lake Erie (was, were) interesting. _____

5. We (was, were) happy viewing the lake. _____

Write *has* or *have* to complete each sentence correctly.

6. We _____ read books about the ocean.

7. Jack _____ written a report on rivers.

8. My friends _____ worked hard on their desert project.

9. The librarian _____ shown me books on mountains.

10. I _____ found pictures of tall mountains for my report.

37

Name _____ Date _____

Spelling the /k/ and /kw/ Sounds

Write the Basic Word that best replaces the underlined word or words in each sentence.

1. The recipe called for <u>four cups</u> of milk.

2. The mouse let out a <u>high, little sound</u> and then ran away.

3. The <u>little piece</u> of snow melted as soon as it touched my warm skin.

4. This is the <u>chilliest</u> winter day we have had this year.

5. Will you <u>look over</u> my report for spelling mistakes?

6. We have tickets to go to the <u>fun show in the big tent</u>!

7. With one <u>fast</u> kick, the player scored the winning goal.

8. When the king died, the <u>king's wife</u> became the country's leader.

9. Hold the egg carefully so that it won't <u>break open</u>.

10. My baby sister likes to grab my finger and <u>hold tightly to</u> it.

1. _____   6. _____

2. _____   7. _____

3. _____   8. _____

4. _____   9. _____

5. _____   10. _____

Spelling Words
Basic
1. shark
2. check
3. queen
4. circus
5. flake
6. crack
7. second
8. squeeze
9. quart
10. squeak
11. quick
12. coldest
13. Africa
14. Mexico
Review
black
thank
Challenge
correct
question

Challenge: On a separate sheet of paper, write a sentence using each Challenge Word. Then rewrite your sentences replacing each Challenge Word with a synonym. Use a dictionary or thesaurus if you need help.

Name _____ Date _____

Lesson 18
READER'S NOTEBOOK

A Tree Is Growing
Vocabulary Strategies:
Word Roots

Word Roots

Identify the root and tell its meaning. Use the meaning of the root to figure out the meaning of the word.

1. telephone
Root:
Meaning of the root:
Meaning of the word:

2. telescope
Root:
Meaning of the root:
Meaning of the word:

3. autocorrect
Root:
Meaning of the root:
Meaning of the word:

4. autopilot
Root:
Meaning of the root:
Meaning of the word:

5. automatic
Root:
Meaning of the root:
Meaning of the word:

Name _____ Date _____

Lesson 18
READER'S NOTEBOOK

A Tree Is Growing
Grammar:
Spiral Review

Abstract Nouns

- Nouns are words that name people, places, or things.
- **Abstract nouns** name things that *cannot* be seen, touched, heard, smelled, or tasted.

  idea   energy   growth   happiness

  Mira had a good <u>idea</u> about saving <u>energy</u>.

  The <u>growth</u> of my plants fills me with <u>happiness</u>.

Thinking Question
Can I see, touch, hear, smell, or taste it?

Write the abstract noun in each sentence.

1. Fear stopped him from opening the door. _____

2. Ben's disappointment made him very quiet. _____

3. The puppy barked with joy. _____

4. Jan had the freedom to pick her own books. _____

5. Jill was filled with relief when she found her lost hamster.

_____

Proofreading for Spelling

Find the misspelled words and circle them.

Dear Sam,

   I am having a great time in Mexico. On the
seckond day of our trip, Dad took me snorkeling.
I had to wear a wetsuit because the water here is
the koldest I've ever felt! Before we got in the
water, Dad called the beach patrol to ask a very
important qwestion. He had to chek and makc
sure there was no sharck danger!

   Snorkeling was fun. We saw all kinds of fish. I
even saw one called a clownfish. It was as colorful
as a real circkus clown! Dad pointed out a fish
trying to catch a little squid. We watched the
squid scueeze out black ink. Then it madc a quik
getaway. It was amazing to see!

   Today my parents and I went to the market.
We used some of the Spanish words we've learned.
People smile and try to understand us even when
we don't say things the korrect way. Sometimes
we get the words all mixed up and just crac up
laughing.

   We are having a lot of fun. I hope you are
having fun back at home. I'll see you in a few days.
                              Your friend,
                              Mark

Spelling Words

Basic
1. shark
2. check
3. queen
4. circus
5. flake
6. crack
7. second
8. squeeze
9. quart
10. squeak
11. quick
12. coldest
13. Africa
14. Mexico

Review
black
thank

Challenge
correct
question

**On a separate sheet of paper, write the misspelled words
correctly.**

Connect to Writing

Short Sentences	Longer, Smoother Sentence
Mount Whitney is very high. White Mountain is very high.	Mount Whitney and White Mountain are very high.
Elise has hiked in the woods. Jamik has hiked in the woods.	Elise and Jamik have hiked in the woods.

Combine two short sentences by moving one subject to make one longer sentence with two subjects. Write the new sentence on the line. Be sure to change the forms of the verbs to match the subject of the new sentence.

1. A goat lives in the mountains. A wolf lives in the mountains.

_____

2. A hiker has stopped at the ranger station. A camper has stopped at the ranger station.

_____

3. My aunt likes hiking in the woods. My uncle likes hiking in the woods.

_____

4. Ellen has reached the top of the mountain. Steven has reached the top of the mountain.

_____

5. Ali was on the bridge. Jane was on the bridge.

_____

Vowel Sounds in
spoon and *wood*

**Read each sentence. Choose the missing word from the box.
Write the word. Then reread the complete sentence.**

hooded	juicy	screws
sunroof	reduce	shouldn't
clue	youth	rules

1. Max hid a present for his mother and left a very good _____ about where to look for it.

2. To help the environment, we are trying to _____ the amount of trash we create.

3. We should use _____, not nails, to put the birdhouse together.

4. The large dog stuck his head out the _____ when his owner took him for a ride in the sports car.

5. My grandfather likes to tell stories about what life was like in his

   _____.

6. Before the game, the umpire reminded us to play by the

   _____.

7. You _____ run when the sidewalk is slippery.

8. Dad told me to wear my _____ jacket to keep my ears warm.

9. The _____ watermelon dripped on my shirt.

Come, Do, Go, Run, and See

The verbs **come**, **do**, **go**, **run**, and **see** are irregular and have special spellings to show past tense. These verbs may also have other spellings when they are used with *has*, *had*, or *have*.

A mouse had <u>gone</u> into our house.

The mouse <u>ran</u> into the woods yesterday.

Thinking Questions
Is the verb in the past tense? Is the verb used with has, have, *or* had?

Write the correct past tense of the verb in parentheses to complete each sentence.

1. My sister had (went, gone) outside. _____

2. Tammy (saw, seen) the mouse in a pile of leaves. _____

3. My brother has (ran, run) outside, too. _____

4. Our neighbors had (saw, seen) the mouse on the bird feeder.

   _____

5. The mice also (did, done) some damage to some feed bags.

   _____

6. They have (ran, run) through the gardens. _____

7. The baby mice (go, went) into the nest. _____

8. I (did, done) a drawing of a mouse last night.

   _____

Eat, Give, Grow, Take, and *Write*

Thinking Questions
Is the verb in the past tense? Is the verb used with has, have, *or* had?

The verbs **eat**, **give**, **grow**, **take**, and **write** have special spellings to show past tense. These verbs also have other spellings when they are used with *has*, *had*, and *have*.

My mother <u>gave</u> me a book about bears.

The author has <u>written</u> books about other animals.

Write the correct past tense of the verb in parentheses to complete each sentence.

1. I (wrote, written) my name on the cover of my book. _____

2. The first chapter (gave, given) facts about bears. _____

3. I have (took, taken) the book to my friend's house. _____

4. She (gave, given) me a book about mountain lions. _____

5. She had (wrote, written) her name in her book, too. _____

6. Her dog had (ate, eaten) a corner of the book. _____

7. That dog has (grew, grown) a lot this year! _____

8. I (ate, eaten) a cookie before leaving. _____

Vowel Sounds in *spoon* and *wood*

Write each Basic Word under the correct heading.

Vowel Sounds in *spoon*	Vowel Sounds in *wood*
_____	_____
_____	_____
_____	_____
_____	_____
_____	_____
_____	_____
_____	_____
_____	_____
_____	_____
_____	_____
_____	_____
_____	_____
_____	_____

Spelling Words

Basic
1. mood
2. wooden
3. drew
4. smooth
5. blue
6. balloon
7. true
8. crooked
9. chew
10. tooth
11. hooves
12. cool
13. food
14. pooch

Review
blew
foot

Challenge
loose
jewel

Challenge: Add the Challenge Words to your Word Sort.

Focus Trait: Purpose
Thinking About Your Audience

> Good writers ask, "What reasons will convince my audience to agree with me?"
>
> Marla is writing to convince her parents to let her go on a class trip to the zoo. Marla brainstormed reasons. Then she chose the ones that her audience, her parents, would care most about.
>
> • She can learn many things about animals, such as bears, at the zoo.
>
> • The teacher, principal, and five other parents will be on the trip.
>
> • She will promise to follow safety rules.

Read about each writer and his or her purpose. Underline the reason that the writer's audience would care most about. Then add another reason that the audience would care about.

1. Jovan is writing to convince his older brother to follow their mother's rules.

   A. When we follow Mother's rules, she is happier.

   B. Mother likes to go to the gym in the afternoons while we are at school.

   Another reason: _____

2. Stephanie is writing to convince her father to let her join the soccer team.

   A. Soccer is one of the most popular sports in the world.

   B. Soccer is great exercise, and lots of players make new friends.

   Another reason: _____

Name _____ Date _____

Lesson 19
READER'S NOTEBOOK

Two Bear Cubs
Phonics:
Cumulative Review

Cumulative Review

Choose a word from the box to complete each sentence.
Write the word on the line. Then read the sentence.

shampoo	woof	lookout
chewing	clues	food

1. In comic strips, dogs often say "arf" or "_____."

2. To keep its owner safe, a guide dog is always on the
   _____.

3. Some dogs use their noses to find _____ about the
   right trail to follow.

4. Most grown dogs eat twice a day, but puppies need _____
   four times a day.

5. Dogs should be washed with _____ made just for dogs.
   Try not to get the suds in the dog's eyes.

6. Sometimes a dog enjoys _____ on a special treat to
   keep its teeth healthy and strong.

Reader's Guide

Two Bear Cubs

Write a Theater Review

Write a review of *Two Bear Cubs* for your local newspaper. First, use details from the text and illustrations to gather information about the play.

Read pages 134–136. Describe the setting and main characters.

_____

_____

Read page 137. How does the end of Scene 1 change the story?

_____

_____

Read pages 139–143. What happens in Scene 2? How does it end?

_____

_____

Read pages 145–149. Who is the hero of Scene 3? Why?

_____

_____

Read page 151. What is the message at the very end of the play?

_____

_____

Name _____ Date _____

Now use all the details from the previous page to write your review. Include the characters, the setting, and the plot. At the end, be sure to say whether you liked the play and why.

A Review of *Two Bear Cubs*

Come, Do, Go, Run, See, Eat, Give, Grow, Take, and Write

Write the correct past tense of the verb in parentheses to complete each sentence.

1. The class (go, went) to the play downtown. _____

2. Some parents (come, came) with us last year. _____

3. The actors have (grow, grown) stronger since last year. _____

4. One person (took, taken) her camera to the play. _____

5. We have (wrote, written) about the play for class. _____

Write the correct past-tense form of the verb in parentheses to complete the sentence.

6. In the play, actors _____ their best to please the crowd. (do)

7. The actors pretended to have _____ a huge feast. (eat)

8. A friend _____ to my seat during the play. (come)

9. He _____ a few pictures with his camera. (take)

10. We have _____ some interesting plays this year. (see)

Vowel Sounds in *spoon* and *wood*

Use the Basic Words to complete the puzzle.

Spelling Words

Basic
1. mood
2. wooden
3. drew
4. smooth
5. blue
6. balloon
7. true
8. crooked
9. chew
10. tooth
11. hooves
12. cool
13. food
14. pooch

Review
blew
foot

Challenge
loose
jewel

Across

2. used to bite
3. to eat
7. not straight
8. what you eat
10. It is filled with air.

Down

1. small dog
4. made of boards
5. traced or sketched
6. opposite of warm
9. feeling

Prefixes *pre-*, *re-*, *bi-*

In each sentence, circle the word with the prefix
pre-, *re-*, or *bi-*. Then write the base word, the prefix,
and the word meaning.

1. My mom can fix just about anything that goes wrong on a bicycle.

   _____   _____   _____
   base word   **prefix**   **meaning**

2. I always go get popcorn during the previews at the movies.

   _____   _____   _____
   base word   **prefix**   **meaning**

3. Jenna liked the book so much that she reread it three times.

   _____   _____   _____
   base word   **prefix**   **meaning**

4. Hector and I meet biweekly to work on our social studies project.

   _____   _____   _____
   base word   **prefix**   **meaning**

5. Our class visited a museum to see an exhibit of prehistoric art.

   _____   _____   _____
   base word   **prefix**   **meaning**

Pronoun-Verb Agreement

- Add *-s* or *-es* to a verb in the present tense when the pronoun in the subject is *he*, *she*, or *it*.
- Do not add *-s* or *-es* to a verb in the present tense when the pronoun in the subject is *I*, *you*, *we*, or *they*.
- Change the *y* to *i* and add *-es* to form the present tense of verbs that end with *y* when the subject is *he*, *she*, or *it*.

  I <u>toss</u> the ball.   I <u>fly</u> kites.

  She <u>splashes</u> into the lake.   She <u>flies</u> kites.

Write the correct verb in parentheses to go with each underlined subject.

1. <u>He</u> (drive, drives) to the theater. _____

2. <u>We</u> (watch, watches) the actors. _____

3. <u>They</u> (perform, performs) really well. _____

4. <u>She</u> (study, studies) acting. _____

Combine each pair of sentences. Change the underlined words to pronouns. Write the new sentences on the lines.

5. Aunt Clara goes to plays. <u>Aunt Clara</u> goes to concerts, too.

_____

6. A bus takes them to the theater. <u>A bus</u> brings them back, too.

_____

Proofreading for Spelling

Find and circle the misspelled words.

Dear Grandma,

    Thank you for the wonderful day at the petting zoo. It put me in such a good moud. I remember hearing hooves as we walked across the wuden bridge. Seeing a mule up close was cule! I liked feeding it hay to chue.

    It was fun to feed the animals handfuls of their special fuud. I liked petting the deer's smoath fur. I think the lamb smiled at me. It had a cute crooked tooth!

    I really like the blue ballone you got me. It reminds me of our fun day. I droo a picture that I am sending to you. It shows you, me, the lamb, the mule, and the black pooch we saw. It is true that this day was the best one ever!

                  Love,

                  Quinn

Spelling Words

Basic
1. mood
2. wooden
3. drew
4. smooth
5. blue
6. balloon
7. true
8. crooked
9. chew
10. tooth
11. hooves
12. cool
13. food
14. pooch

Review
blew
foot

Challenge
loose
jewel

Write the misspelled words correctly on the lines below.

1. _____   5. _____

2. _____   6. _____

3. _____   7. _____

4. _____   8. _____

Connect to Writing

Using exact verbs helps the reader better picture what you are describing in your writing.

Less Exact Verb	More Exact Verb
run	sprint, jog, dash, race
talk	whisper, chatter, gossip, debate

For each verb, write a sentence that shows its exact meaning.
Use a dictionary if you need help.

1. sprint

_____

_____

2. jog

_____

_____

3. dash

_____

_____

4. race

_____

_____

5. whisper

_____

_____

Name _____ Date _____

Lesson 20
READER'S NOTEBOOK

Life on the Ice
Phonics:
Compound Words

Compound Words

Write a word from the box to answer each clue. Then answer
the question below by reading the word in the shaded boxes.

chalkboard	flashlight	outside	toothbrush
cookbook	homework	snowshoes	underwater
fireplace	newspaper		

1.

2.

3.

4.

5.

6.

7.

8.

9.

10.

1. This helps you see in the dark.

2. You wear these to walk in snow.

3. You need this to brush your teeth.

4. Look here to see fish in a lake.

5. You do this work after school.

6. This is a book of recipes.

7. You might play here after school.

8. A fire in here will warm a room.

9. A teacher may write on this in a classroom.

10. You read this to learn the news.

What is the coldest place on Earth? _____

Adverbs That Tell *How*

- Words that describe verbs are called **adverbs**.

- Adverbs can tell *how* an action happens. Most adverbs that tell *how* end in *-ly*.

- Adverbs can come before or after the verbs they describe.

    Lynne <u>happily</u> went skating.

    The skaters moved <u>smoothly</u> across the ice.

Thinking Question
What word tells how?

Write the adverb that tells about the underlined verb in each sentence.

1. They <u>tied</u> their laces tightly. _____

2. Lynne and Lamont <u>moved</u> cautiously at first. _____

3. Lamont <u>watched</u> the skaters carefully. _____

4. Then he <u>skated</u> effortlessly around the rink. _____

5. Proudly, Lynne <u>spun</u> on the ice. _____

6. Lynne's lace <u>broke</u> unexpectedly. _____

7. Slowly, she <u>moved</u> to a bench. _____

8. She <u>arrived</u> at the bench safely. _____

Adverbs That Tell *Where* and *When*

- **Adverbs** can tell *how* an action happens. They can also tell *where* and *when* something happens.
- Adverbs can come before or after the verbs they describe.

Thinking Question
What word tells where or when?

The scientists flew <u>there</u> in an airplane.
<u>Then</u> they cleaned the airplane.

Write the adverb that tells about each underlined verb. Then write
where **or** *when* **to show how each adverb describes the verb.**

1. It's too snowy to <u>leave</u> tonight.   _____

2. First, we will <u>make</u> a shelter.   _____

3. Then we will <u>drink</u> hot chocolate.   _____

4. We can <u>build</u> a shelter there.   _____

5. We will <u>ride</u> snowmobiles tomorrow.   _____

6. We can <u>skate</u> nearby.   _____

7. They <u>hiked</u> away, but then they came back.   _____

8. The iceberg <u>lies</u> ahead.   _____

Name _____ Date _____

Lesson 20
READER'S NOTEBOOK

Life on the Ice
Spelling:
Compound Words

Spelling Word Sort

Read each Basic Word. Listen to the number of syllables.
Write each word under the correct heading.

Words with Two Syllables	Words with Three Syllables
_____	_____
_____	_____
_____	_____
_____	_____
_____	_____
_____	_____
_____	_____
_____	_____
_____	_____
_____	_____

Spelling Words

Basic
1. birthday
2. anyone
3. sometimes
4. everything
5. homework
6. afternoon
7. airplane
8. grandmother
9. something
10. without
11. himself
12. faraway
13. sunburned
14. daylight

Review
someone
cannot

Challenge
scorekeeper
everybody

Review: Add the Review Words to your Word Sort.

Challenge: Which Challenge Word has four syllables?

_____

Add the other Challenge Word to your Word Sort.

Focus Trait: Organization

Paragraphs for Reasons

Good writers make a separate paragraph for each reason in a persuasive essay.

Reasons Together	*Reasons in Paragraphs*
In Antarctica, scientists can learn about pollution. For example, they can find ash from Mount Vesuvius. They learn about how the climate is changing. They can see how quickly ice is melting.	In Antarctica, scientists can learn about pollution. For example, they can find ash from Mount Vesuvius. Additionally, they learn about how the climate is changing. They can see how quickly ice is melting.

Rewrite the following paragraph so that each reason has its own paragraph. Add linking words between paragraphs.

A century ago, explorers built huts in Antarctica. Today, the huts are falling apart. We should save the huts because they are an important part of history. The huts are full of food and clothing. These items can teach us what the explorers' lives were like. The huts are full of books. By reading them, we can learn how explorers prepared for their trip.

_____

_____

_____

_____

_____

61

Cumulative Review

Read each sentence. Choose two words from the Word Bank to form a compound word to complete each sentence. Then read the complete sentence.

bare	brush	eye	sun
bath	brow	fire	room
boat	butter	fly	sail
glasses	camp	foot	paint

1. When you do not have a shoe or sock on your foot, you

   are _____.

2. You use _____ to protect your eyes.

3. To make a colorful picture, you use a _____.

4. The hair that grows just above your eye is called an

   _____.

5. You take a shower in a room called a _____.

6. An insect that uses its pretty wings to fly from flower to

   flower is called a _____.

7. A boat that uses wind and sails is called a

   _____.

8. When you want to cook something while you are

   camping, you build a _____.

Reader's Guide

Life on the Ice

A Travel Guide to the Poles

Gather information about the North and South Poles.
Use the information to create a travel guide.

Read pages 170–171. Where are the Poles? What are they like?

_____

_____

Read pages 174–175. What is traveling to the Poles like?

_____

_____

Read pages 180–181. How do you need to dress at the Poles?

_____

_____

Read pages 182–183. What are the different seasons like for people who live at the Poles?

_____

_____

Name _____ Date _____

Now use the information you collected to design a travel guide for the North and South Poles. Be sure to point out interesting details that would make visitors eager to go. Remember to let your excitement show!

Come to the North and South Poles! An adventure awaits you!

_____

_____

_____

_____

_____

_____

_____

_____

_____

_____

_____

_____

_____

Name _____ Date _____

Lesson 20
READER'S NOTEBOOK

Life on the Ice
Grammar:
What Is an Adverb?

Adverbs That Tell *How*, *Where*, and *When*

Write the adverb that tells *how* the underlined verb happened.

1. The airplane noisily <u>landed</u> on the runway. _____

2. The engines <u>roared</u> loudly as we waited. _____

3. Cheerfully, we <u>waved</u> at the scientists. _____

4. The pilots sternly <u>nodded</u> at us. _____

Write the adverb that describes the underlined verb. Then write *where* or *when* to show how each adverb describes the verb.

5. First, we <u>showed</u> the scientists their rooms. _____

6. We <u>talked</u> with them inside. _____

7. We <u>walked</u> upstairs for a snack. _____

8. Another group <u>arrives</u> tomorrow. _____

Spelling Compound Words

Life on the Ice
Spelling:
Compound Words

Read each book title. Add a Basic Word to complete each title.

Spelling Words

Basic

1. *Teacher, My Dog Ate My* _____!

2. *Using Sunblock to Avoid Getting* _____

3. *Happy* _____, *Rosalinda!*

4. *Sixteen Hours of* _____

5. *Traveling in an* _____

6. *Scott's* _____ *Pen Pal*

7. *Spending the Summer with* _____
   and Grandpa

8. *An* _____ *at the Zoo*

9. *In the Rain* _____ *an Umbrella*

10. *Does* _____ *Know What Time It Is?*

Basic
1. birthday
2. anyone
3. sometimes
4. everything
5. homework
6. afternoon
7. airplane
8. grandmother
9. something
10. without
11. himself
12. faraway
13. sunburned
14. daylight

Review
someone
cannot

Challenge
scorekeeper
everybody

Review: Choose a Review Word. Use it in a book title.

_____

Challenge: Choose a Challenge Word. Use it in a book title.

_____

Name _____ Date _____

Lesson 20
READER'S NOTEBOOK

Life on the Ice
Vocabulary Strategies:
Dictionary/Glossary

Dictionary/Glossary

Read each word. Write the base word to use to find its dictionary entry. Then find each entry word in a dictionary. Write the words with all their endings.

Word	Entry Word in Dictionary	Part(s) of Speech	Word with Endings
1. gliding			
2. hesitate			
3. dripping			
4. rippling			
5. horrifying			

Now write a sentence for one form of each word.

1. _____

_____

2. _____

_____

3. _____

_____

4. _____

_____

5. _____

_____

Simple Verb Tenses

- A verb that tells about an action that has already happened shows **past tense.** Add *-ed* to most verbs to show past tense.

- A verb that tells about an action happening now shows **present tense.** Add *-s* to the verb when the noun in the subject of a sentence is singular. Do not add *-s* to the verb when the noun in the subject is *I, you,* or a plural.

- A verb that tells about an action that will happen in the future shows **future tense.** Use the helping verb *will* for verbs in the future tense.

Write the correct past tense of the verb in parentheses.

1. They _____ to get inside. (hurry)

2. The snow _____ after two hours. (stop)

Write the correct present tense of the verb in parentheses.

3. The girl _____ in the snow. (play)

4. The adults _____ for the skaters. (clap)

Write the correct future tense of the verb in parentheses.

5. We _____ the snow from the steps. (sweep)

6. The snow _____ when the sun comes up. (melt)

Proofreading for Spelling

Read the following letter. Circle the misspelled words.

Dear Grandmoter,

Thank you for my bithday card. It came in the mail this afternown. I love everthing you send me.

I wish you didn't live in such a farawy place. Sumtimes I wish I had an airplan. I would fly to see you all the time. I could be back home whcn it was still daylitc.

Yesterday, I came home from school and played outside. I got sunberned. I canot play outside today. I have a lot of homwork to do.

I can't say goodbye withowt saying I love you and I miss you. I hope you can come see us soon!

Love,
Tony

Spelling Words

Basic
1. birthday
2. anyone
3. sometimes
4. everything
5. homework
6. afternoon
7. airplane
8. grandmother
9. something
10. without
11. himself
12. faraway
13. sunburned
14. daylight

Review
someone
cannot

Challenge
scorekeeper
everybody

Write the misspelled words correctly on the lines below.

1. _____   7. _____

2. _____   8. _____

3. _____   9. _____

4. _____   10. _____

5. _____   11. _____

6. _____   12. _____

Name _____ Date _____

Lesson 20
READER'S NOTEBOOK

Life on the Ice
Grammar:
Connect to Writing

Connect to Writing

Short, choppy sentences can be combined to make
your writing smoother. Combine two sentences by moving
an adverb.

Short Sentences	Longer, Smoother Sentences
Sam walked up the hill. The hill was nearby.	Sam walked up the nearby hill.
They wait to skate. They wait eagerly.	They wait eagerly to skate.

Combine two short, choppy sentences by moving the adverb.
Write the sentence.

1. We rode our sleds. We rode today.

   _____

2. I screamed as I flew downhill. I screamed loudly.

   _____

3. I ran back up the hill. I ran eagerly.

   _____

4. I reached the top. I reached it first.

   _____

Name _____ Date _____

Unit 4
READER'S NOTEBOOK

Boy, Were We Wrong
About Dinosaurs!
Segment 1
Independent Reading

Reader's Guide

Boy, Were We Wrong About Dinosaurs!

An Ancient Chinese Scroll

Imagine you were in ancient China and helped find the giant bones! You will write on a Chinese scroll to explain what you saw. First, answer some questions that will help you write about your findings.

Read pages 4–6. How were the first dinosaur bones found?

_____

_____

Why did wise men think the bones came from dragons?

_____

_____

Why didn't they know the bones came from dinosaurs?

_____

_____

How do you think the men in ancient China felt once they discovered the huge bones?

_____

_____

Name _____ Date _____

Unit 4
READER'S NOTEBOOK

Boy, Were We Wrong About Dinosaurs!
Segment 1
Independent Reading

Now use your answers to write a scroll. Tell how you found the bones. Tell what you thought they were. Tell how you felt about your find.

_____

_____

_____

_____

_____

_____

_____

_____

_____

_____

_____

_____

_____

_____

_____

_____

Name _____ Date _____

Unit 4
READER'S NOTEBOOK

Boy, Were We Wrong About Dinosaurs!
Segment 1
Independent Reading

Then and Now Pictures

Scientists had some wrong ideas about dinosaurs!
Draw pictures that show how scientists' ideas about
dinosours have changed. First, use the text and
illustrations to answer the questions below.

**Read page 8. What did scientists first think about the
horn-shaped bone of the iguanodon?**

_____

_____

**Read page 9. What did scientists realize later about the
horn-shaped bone?**

_____

_____

**Read page 10. What did scientists first think about the elbows
and knees of dinosaurs?**

_____

_____

How did scientists first think that dinosaurs moved?

_____

_____

Unit 4
READER'S NOTEBOOK

**Boy, Were We Wrong
About Dinosaurs!**
Segment 1
Independent Reading

Now use your answers to draw two pictures of an iguanadon. First, draw what scientists used to think they looked like. Next, draw what scientists now believe. Write captions to explain your drawings.

Iguanodon Then

_____

_____

Iguanodon Now

_____

_____

Name _____ Date _____

Unit 4
READER'S NOTEBOOK

Boy, Were We Wrong About Dinosaurs!
Segment 1
Independent Reading

Now answer some questions about dinosaurs' tails.
You will use your answers to draw more Then and
Now pictures.

Read page 12. What did scientists think about dinosaurs' tails?

_____

_____

What evidence made them believe that?

_____

_____

_____

**Read page 13. Now what do scientists think that dinosaurs
did with their tails?**

_____

_____

_____

What clues helped them to realize this?

_____

_____

_____

Name _____ Date _____

First, draw what scientists used to think about dinosaurs' tails. Next, draw what scientists now believe about their tails. Write captions to explain your drawings.

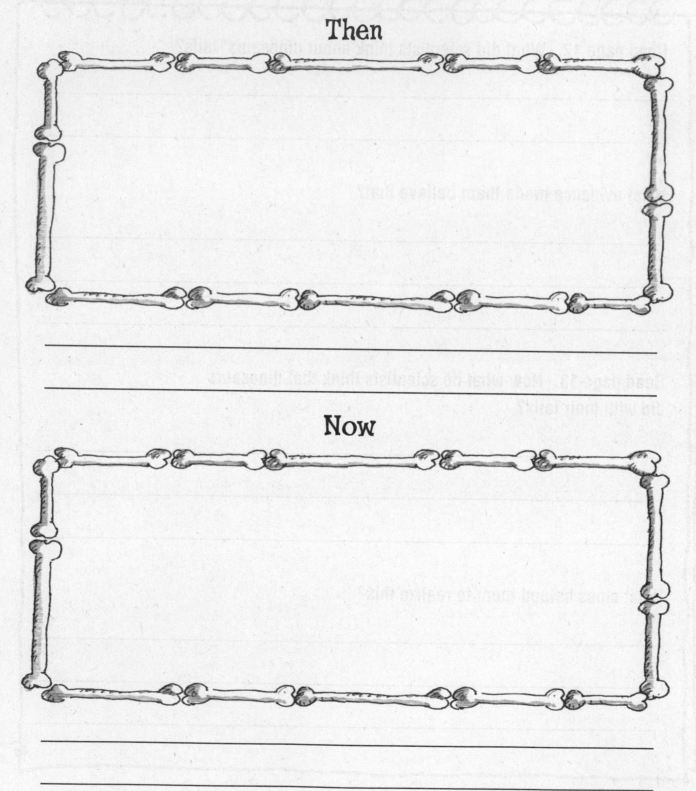

Then

_____

_____

Now

_____

_____

Name _____ Date _____

Unit 4
READER'S NOTEBOOK

Boy, Were We Wrong About Dinosaurs!
Segment 2
Independent Reading

Boy, Were We Wrong About Dinosaurs!

A Letter to the Past

You are going to send a letter in a time machine!
The letter will go to scientists who worked and
lived hundreds of years ago. What will you tell
them about dinosaurs? First, gather facts
from the text. Then, write your letter.

**Read page 14. How did scientists think dinosaurs were
like lizards?**

_____

_____

_____

What do lizard bones look like inside?

_____

_____

_____

How do dinosaur bones compare with lizard bones?

_____

_____

_____

Name _____ Date _____

Unit 4
READER'S NOTEBOOK

Boy, Were We Wrong About Dinosaurs!
Segment 2
Independent Reading

Read page 15. How do scientists think dinosaurs were like birds?

_____

_____

_____

Read pages 16–18. Why do scientists think big dinosaurs did not have fur or feathers?

_____

_____

Read page 19. Why do scientists think little dinosaurs had feathers?

_____

_____

Read page 20. What do scientists now think about the colors of dinosaurs?

_____

_____

_____

Name _____ Date _____

Now use this information to write a letter to scientists of the past. Explain in this letter what we now know about the bones, blood, feathers, and colors of dinosaurs.

Dear Scientists of the Past,

Sincerely yours,

Name _____ Date _____

Unit 4
READER'S NOTEBOOK

Boy, Were We Wrong About Dinosaurs!
Segment 2
Independent Reading

Look Under the Microscope

Suppose you are the leader of a group of scientists who are digging up dinosaur bones. When your group has gathered all the fossils you need, you will be looking at the fossils under a microscope. Draw and label everything you find. Then write a lab report.

Read page 14. You have just found a dinosaur bone and sliced it open. Draw and label what you see under the microscope.

_____

_____

_____

_____

Read page 16. You have just found a fossil with some marks that look like feathers. Draw and label what you see under the microscope.

_____

_____

_____

_____

Name _____ Date _____

Unit 4
READER'S NOTEBOOK

**Boy, Were We Wrong
About Dinosaurs!**
Segment 2
Independent Reading

Read page 18. You have just found the skin of a large dinosaur. Is it smooth or bumpy? Does it have feathers or fur? Draw and label what you see under the microscope.

_____
_____
_____
_____

Read page 19. Now you have found the skin of a small dinosaur. Is it smooth or bumpy? Does it have feathers or fur? Draw and label what you see under the microscope.

_____
_____
_____
_____

Name _____ Date _____

Unit 4
READER'S NOTEBOOK

**Boy, Were We Wrong
About Dinosaurs!**
Segment 2
Independent Reading

Now use what you saw under the microscope to write a lab report. Describe your discoveries about the different parts of dinosaurs.

Lab Report

_____

_____

_____

_____

_____

_____

_____

_____

_____

_____

_____

_____

_____

_____

Name _____   Date _____

Unit 4
READER'S NOTEBOOK
Boy, Were We Wrong
About Dinosaurs!
Segment 3
Independent Reading

Boy, Were We Wrong About Dinosaurs!

Dinosaur Short Story

After reading this book, you know a lot about
baby dinosaurs! Use the text and illustrations to write
a short story about a baby dinosaur. First, answer the
questions below to get the main details.

**Read pages 22–23. What is the same about dinosaur babies
and lizard babies?**

_____

_____

What is different about dinosaur babies and lizard babies?

_____

_____

_____

Read page 24. What did the nests of dinosaurs tell us about them?

_____

_____

What did fossil footprints of dinosaurs tell us about dinosaur babies?

_____

_____

Name _____ Date _____

Unit 4
READER'S NOTEBOOK

**Boy, Were We Wrong
About Dinosaurs!**
Segment 3
Independent Reading

Now write your story about a baby dinosaur.
You can include details about how the baby
was born, how the mother took care of it,
and how it traveled with its family.

_____

_____

_____

_____

_____

_____

_____

_____

_____

_____

_____

_____

_____

_____

_____

Unit 4
READER'S NOTEBOOK

**Boy, Were We Wrong
About Dinosaurs!**
Segment 3
Independent Reading

Draw a Comic Strip

Scientist had many different ideas about what killed off
the dinosaurs. Use the text and illustrations to draw a
comic strip showing what you think might have happened.
The questions below will help you think of some ideas.

Read page 26. What did scientists first think killed off the dinosaurs?

_____

_____

**Why did scientists change their minds about what killed off
the dinosaurs?**

_____

_____

_____

Read page 27. Why would dinosaurs die if the sun was blocked?

_____

_____

_____

Name _____ Date _____

Unit 4
READER'S NOTEBOOK

Boy, Were We Wrong About Dinosaurs!
Segment 3
Independent Reading

Now draw a comic strip showing how scientists think the dinosaurs died.

Name _____ Date _____

Unit 4
READER'S NOTEBOOK

Boy, Were We Wrong
About Dinosaurs!
Segment 3
Independent Reading

Write a Speech

We may still be wrong about the dinosaurs. Scientists keep making discoveries. Be a scientist! You have just made an important discovery about dinosaurs. Plan the speech you are going to give to a group of scientists about your discovery. Then write the speech.

Read pages 22–24. What don't we know about dinosaur babies?

_____

_____

_____

Read pages 26–27. What don't we know about why dinosaurs died?

_____

_____

_____

Read page 29. Why do some scientists believe that some dinosaurs are still alive?

_____

_____

What are some other things we don't know about dinosaurs yet?

_____

_____

Name _____ Date _____

Unit 4
READER'S NOTEBOOK

Boy, Were We Wrong About Dinosaurs!
Segment 3
Independent Reading

Now write your speech about your latest discovery.
You are going to talk to a group of scientists.
Describe the new information you have about
dinosaurs and why you believe it is true.

Name _____ Date _____

Lesson 21
READER'S NOTEBOOK

Sarah, Plain and Tall
Phonics:
Base Words and -ed, -ing

Base Words and *-ed, -ing*

Read each sentence. Choose the missing word from the box.
Write the word. Then reread the complete sentence.

juggling	skipped	sliced
rattled	exciting	practiced
excused	tasting	unzipped

1. Travis _____ his jacket, took it off, and hung
   it up.

2. The two girls _____ across the playground
   instead of walking.

3. The clown is _____ four balls high into
   the air.

4. The polite man _____ himself before he got
   up from the table.

5. "It was _____ to see real giraffes at the zoo!"
   Keisha said.

6. Did your eyes water when you _____ the

   onions?

7. When the snake _____ its tail, we took off
   running.

8. I _____ my spelling words over and over.

9. The chef is _____ the stew to see if it needs
   more salt.

Adverbs That Compare

- **Adverbs** can tell *where, when,* or *how* something happens. Adverbs are used to describe verbs. Adverbs can also be used to compare actions.

- To compare two actions, use the ending *-er* with most adverbs, such as *hard, late,* or *slow*.

- Use *more* before adverbs that end in *-ly,* such as *carefully* or *quickly*.

  > **Thinking Question**
  > *Are two actions compared?*

  She practiced <u>harder</u> than her brother needed to practice.
  She danced <u>more awkwardly</u> than her brother did.

Choose the correct adverb in parentheses. Write it on the line.

1. The brother and sister acted (bashfully, more bashfully) than their father. _____

2. Abby waited (eagerly, more eagerly) than her brother did. _____

3. The woman sang (gently, more gently) than the wind blew. _____

4. She swayed (gracefully, more gracefully) than the prairie grasses moved outside. _____

5. The song sounded (stronger, more stronger) than it did before. _____

6. The little girl held her toy bear (carefully, more carefully) than she would hold a ball. _____

Adverbs That Compare

- **Adverbs** can be used to compare two actions.

- Add *-er* to one-syllable adverbs to show comparison. If the adverb ends with *e*, drop the *e* before adding *-er*.

Thinking Question
Does the adverb have more than one syllable or does it end in -ly?

- Use *more* before adverbs that end in *-ly*. Sometimes, an adverb that ends with *-ly* will use an *-ier* ending.

  The moon shines <u>brighter</u> than the stars.

  Linda could see the moon <u>earlier</u> than she could notice the stars.

  The stars twinkled <u>more brilliantly</u> than the moon glowed.

Write the correct form of the adverb in parentheses to complete the sentence.

1. The truck arrived (late) today than the bus did.

_____

2. The cornstalks stood (rigidly) than the tall grass.

_____

3. She watched the sheep (closely) than she watched the cows. _____

4. They climbed (high) than we could.

_____

5. The wind is blowing (strong) now than it did this morning.

_____

Spelling Word Sort

Write each Basic Word under the correct heading.

Words with *-ed*	Words with *-ing*

Review: Add the Review Words to your Word Sort.

Challenge: Add the Challenge Words to your Word Sort.

Spelling Words

Basic
1. coming
2. swimming
3. dropping
4. tapping
5. taping
6. invited
7. saving
8. stared
9. planned
10. changing
11. joking
12. loved
13. gripped
14. tasted

Review
making
stopped

Challenge
freezing
scared

Focus Trait: Development
Setting the Scene

Setting the scene means telling the reader who the main character or narrator is and what is happening as the story begins.

The chart below lists questions that a writer answers to set the scene. Read the example answers, and then complete the chart with answers of your own.

Questions	Example Answers	Your Answers
Who is the main character or narrator?	a young scientist	
What is he or she doing?	She is studying elephants, and she has found an injured baby elephant.	
Where and when are events taking place?	Events take place in the rain forest in Africa. It is early in the morning.	
What problem does the main character or narrator face?	The scientist must take care of the baby and bring it to an animal refuge.	

Cumulative Review

**Read each sentence. Choose the missing word from the box.
Write the word. Then reread the complete sentence.**

chopped	haircut	tripped
described	included	watermelon
driveway	racing	
driving	spinning	

1. The man admired his new short _____ in the mirror.

2. In the dark, Lee Ann _____ and fell over a chair.

3. Martin _____ the carrot into small pieces.

4. Mr. Ward parked his truck in the _____.

5. The puppy is _____ in a circle, chasing its tail!

6. A cap is _____ as part of your baseball uniform.

7. We ate juicy _____ at the school picnic.

8. Braden _____ every detail of the painting.

9. It was fun to watch the two squirrels _____ up and down the tree.

10. I saw an electric car _____ past our school.

Reader's Guide

Sarah, Plain and Tall

Write in Caleb's Diary

Help complete Caleb's diary entries with details from the story.

Read pages 209–211. How did Caleb feel before Sarah arrived?

Dear Diary,

_____

Read pages 213–215. What was it like when Caleb met Sarah?

Dear Diary,

_____

**Read page 216. How did Sarah feel about living with the family?
What did this make Caleb think?**

Dear Diary,

_____

_____

Read pages 217–218. How did Caleb feel when he and Anna picked flowers with Sarah?

Dear Diary,

_____

_____

_____

Read pages 219–220. How did Caleb feel later that evening?

Dear Diary,

_____

_____

_____

Read page 221. What happened at the end of the evening?

Dear Diary,

_____

_____

_____

Name _____ Date _____

Adverbs That Compare

Write the correct form of the adverb that compares more than two actions.

1. easily _____

2. furiously _____

3. late _____

4. perfectly _____

5. rigidly _____

6. high _____

Write the form of the adverb that compares more than two actions in parentheses.

1. Sam worked _____ of all the workers. (slowly)

2. Jim shoveled the _____ of all the adults. (quickly)

3. Sally worked the _____ of the three people on her team. (hard)

4. Jenny always arrived _____ at work. (early)

Name _____ Date _____

Words with *-ed* and *-ing*

Write the Basic Word that replaces the underlined word or words in each book title.

1. <u>Kidding</u> and Laughing _____

2. <u>Moving</u> to California _____

3. Stop <u>Letting Go</u> of the Ball _____

4. <u>Sticking Together</u> and Gluing Projects

_____

5. <u>Moving</u> in Water Sports _____

6. <u>Asked</u> to the Party _____

7. Pets I Have <u>Liked</u> a Lot _____

8. <u>Keeping</u> Money in a Bank _____

9. We <u>Arranged</u> a Party _____

10. <u>Making</u> Different Weather _____

11. He <u>Held</u> a Baseball Bat _____

12. <u>Hitting Lightly</u> at the Door _____

13. Teas I Have <u>Tried</u> _____

14. The Monster <u>Looked</u> at Me! _____

Review What Review Word completes this title?

The Art of _____ Bread

Challenge Write your own title using one of the Challenge Words.

_____

Spelling Words

Basic
1. coming
2. swimming
3. dropping
4. tapping
5. taping
6. invited
7. saving
8. stared
9. planned
10. changing
11. joking
12. loved
13. gripped
14. tasted

Review
making
stopped

Challenge
freezing
scared

Name _____ Date _____

Lesson 21
READER'S NOTEBOOK

Sarah, Plain and Tall
Vocabulary Strategies:
Prefix *non-*

Prefix *non-*

Read each question. Add the prefix *non-* to the underlined word and write a new word. Use the new word to write an answer to each question.

1. A cat is a living thing. What is an example of something that is not <u>living</u>?

   _____

2. Violent storms, such as tornadoes, can occur on the prairie. What kind of a storm is not <u>violent</u>?

   _____

3. Anna and Caleb are productive when they do their chores. During the day, when are you not <u>productive</u>?

   _____

4. Caleb could not stop talking to Sarah. What is something you would like to do and not <u>stop</u>?

   _____

5. *Sarah, Plain and Tall* is fiction. What is your favorite book that is not <u>fiction</u>?

   _____

6. Papa, Anna, and Caleb write letters to Sarah. What is another way of communicating with someone that is not <u>verbal</u>?

   _____

Kinds of Adjectives

Words that describe, or tell about, nouns are called
adjectives. Adjectives can tell **what kind** or **how many**
about a noun.

Jasmine loves <u>sweet</u> foods.

**Write the adjective that tells *what kind* or *how many* about the
underlined noun.**

1. Tara made chocolate <u>cake</u>. _____

2. Our diet has little <u>sugar</u>. _____

3. We eat three <u>kinds</u> of vegetables. _____

4. We drink many <u>glasses</u> of water daily. _____

5. My mother makes healthful <u>meals</u>. _____

**Combine each pair of sentences. In the new sentence, use two
adjectives to describe the same noun.**

6. The vegetables are healthful. The vegetables are delicious.

   _____

7. The pie was sweet. It was also juicy.

   _____

8. The drink was thick. It was icy, too.

   _____

Proofreading for Spelling

Read the following invitation. Find and circle the
misspelled words.

Spelling Words

Basic
1. coming
2. swimming
3. dropping
4. tapping
5. taping
6. invited
7. saving
8. stared
9. planned
10. changing
11. joking
12. loved
13. gripped
14. tasted

Review
making
stopped

Challenge
freezing
scared

You Are Invited To A Swiming Party!

Parents will be droping kids at the planed
meeting place: the changging rooms at Bayview
Park. Everyone is coming at 11:00.

I have been saveing plastic flowers. We will be
tapeing them onto our bathing caps. People stared
when we did this at my sister's party. I think they
all lovved how we looked and knew we were only
jokeing.

We will play in the water until noon. We
griped hands at my sister's party and jumped over
wavcs. Maybe we can do that again! Then my dad
will make a tapping signal. He will serve chicken
and salad for lunch. I've tastted his cooking and it
will be great! Finally, we'll have a second swim. It
will be a fun party. I hope you can make it!

Write the misspelled words correctly on the lines below.

1. _____   6. _____

2. _____   7. _____

3. _____   8. _____

4. _____   9. _____

5. _____   10. _____

Connect to Writing

You can make your ideas clearer by using adverbs that compare. To compare two actions, add *-er* to most adverbs. Use *more* before an adverb that ends in *-ly*. To compare more than two actions, add *-est* to most adverbs. Use *most* before an adverb that ends in *-ly*.

Incorrect Adverb Form	Correct Adverb Form
Mary will arrive soonest than Ellen.	Mary will arrive sooner than Ellen.
The gray kitten acts the more lively of all the cats.	The gray kitten acts the most lively of all the cats.

Use the correct form of the adverb in parentheses. Write the sentence.

1. Ellen ran to the barn (fast) than Mary.

_____

2. Mary climbed the ladder (quickly) than Ellen.

_____

3. The white kitten moved (slow) of all the kittens.

_____

4. The gray kitten cried (loud) than the white kitten.

_____

5. Mary played with the kittens (carefully) than Ellen did.

_____

Spelling Changes: -s, -es, -ed, -ing

Read each sentence. Choose the missing word from the box.
Write the word.   Then reread the complete sentence.

hurried	drying	cities
replied	pennies	grazed
traveled	memories	
pillows	paintbrushes	

1. April _____ to the question with another question.

2. I have such good _____ of kindergarten!

3. Most of the big _____ in California are on the coast.

4. The goats _____ on the hillside.

5. Ten _____ equal one dime.

6. Alexander _____ to school so he wouldn't be late.

7. The class _____ to the zoo on a bus.

8. Joshua broke a plate as he was _____ the dishes.

9. Mom set two fluffy _____ on the bed.

10. The artist had many _____ of different sizes.

Adjectives That Compare

- **Adjectives** are used to describe nouns. Adjectives can also be used to **compare** two or more nouns.

- Add the ending -er to most adjectives to compare two nouns. Add -est to compare more than two nouns.

Adjective	Comparing Two Nouns	Comparing More Than Two Nouns
tall	taller	tallest
high	higher	highest
large	larger	largest

Thinking Question
How many nouns are being compared?

Kim's hair is long. Morgan's hair is longer than Kim's. Jamie's hair is the longest of all.

Write the correct form of the adjective in parentheses.

1. Monarch butterflies are (quick) than turtles.

_____

2. One book showed that the butterfly was (bright) than the flower it landed on. _____

3. The (long) section in the book was about migration.

_____

4. Male monarchs are (big) than female monarchs.

_____

104

Name _____ Date _____

Lesson 22
READER'S NOTEBOOK

The Journey:
Stories of Migration
Grammar:
Making Comparisons

Adverbs That Compare

- **Adverbs** tell *when*, *where*, or *how* something happened.
  They can also be used to **compare actions.**
- Add the ending *-er* to adverbs to compare two actions.
- To compare more than two actions, add the ending *-est.*

Adverb	Comparing Two Actions	Comparing More Than Two Actions
late	later	latest
quickly	more quickly	most quickly
fast	faster	fastest

Thinking Question
How many actions are being compared?

Len jumped high. I jumped higher than Len. Lou jumped the highest of all.

Write the correct form of the adverb in parentheses.

1. I thought the whale swam (fast) than the dolphin. _____

2. Lee thought the dolphins swam the (fast) of all the animals we saw. _____

3. We talked (softly) than we do in school. _____

4. The dolphin dived (deep) than the school of fish. _____

Spelling Word Sort

The Journey:
Stories of Migration
Spelling:
Changing Final *y* to *i*

Write each Basic Word under the correct heading.

Words ending with *-es*	Words ending with *-ed*
_____	_____
_____	_____
_____	_____
_____	_____
_____	_____
_____	_____
_____	_____
_____	_____
_____	_____
_____	_____

Review: Suppose you were asked to add a column for the Review Words. What would you name the heading of that column? _____

Challenge: Add the Challenge Words to your Word Sort.

Spelling Words

Basic
1. cities
2. cried
3. puppies
4. hurried
5. stories
6. flies
7. parties
8. tried
9. pennies
10. fried
11. carried
12. babies
13. spied
14. ponies

Review
pretty
very

Challenge
countries
libraries

Name _____ Date _____

Lesson 22
READER'S NOTEBOOK

The Journey:
Stories of Migration
Writing:
Narrative Writing

Focus Trait: Elaboration
Using Similes

Description	Simile Added
My face turned red.	My face turned as red as a tomato.

A. Read each description. Create a clearer picture by adding a simile using *like* or *as*.

Description	Simile Added
1. Huge rain clouds blocked the sun and made it dark outside.	Huge rain clouds blocked the sun and made _____.
2. The children walking in the hallway are loud.	The children walking in the hallway are _____ _____.

B. Read each description. Add a simile to each description to create a clearer picture for the reader. Write your new sentences.

Description	Simile Added
3. The freshly washed floor was slippery.	
4. The new mall is huge.	

Pair/Share Work with a partner to brainstorm similes to add to each description.

Name _____ Date _____

Lesson 22
READER'S NOTEBOOK

Less Common Plurals

The Journey:
Stories of Migration
Phonics:
Less Common Plurals

Read each sentence. Choose the missing word from
the box. Write the word. Then reread each complete sentence.

knives
leaves
hooves
lives
loaves

1. The blacksmith put shoes on the horses'

   _____.

2. Run for your _____! The volcano is erupting!

3. Do you have any _____ of wheat bread?

4. In autumn, the _____ fall from the trees.

5. Set the table with forks, _____, and spoons.

Name _____ Date _____

Lesson 22
READER'S NOTEBOOK

**The Journey: Stories
of Migration**
Independent Reading

Reader's Guide

The Journey: Stories of Migration

An Interview with Locust and Whale

Hello and welcome to the weekly radio program, *Animal Journeys*. Today we are going to talk with Locust and Whale, two animals that take amazing journeys.

Read pages 241–242. Locust, let's hear your story first. What makes you migrate?

Locust: _____

_____

_____

Read page 243. How interesting. What happens when you all land?

Locust: _____

_____

_____

Read pages 246–247. Now tell us more about how you travel.

Locust: _____

_____

_____

Read pages 248–250. Whale, you migrate too but for different reasons. Why do you migrate?

Whale: _____

_____

What do you do on your migration that is similar to what locusts do?

Whale: _____

_____

Read pages 251–252. When you arrive at the warm tropical waters in January, what happens?

Whale: _____

_____

Read pages 252–253. When spring comes, why do you migrate again?

Whale: _____

_____

Thank you both for joining us on *Animal Journeys*. We have learned a lot today about your journeys across the world!

Adjectives and Adverbs That Compare

Review with students that adjectives compare nouns, and adverbs compare verbs, or actions.

Write an adjective or adverb to complete each sentence. Then write _adjective_ or _adverb_ to identify the answer you gave.

1. A butterfly's wings move _____ than a locust's wings. (quietly) _____

2. Locusts are the _____ of all insects. (hungry) _____

3. The waves splashed _____ than they had earlier in the day. (high) _____

4. The waters near the Arctic are _____ than the waters near Mexico. (cold) _____

Write two sentences. Include an adjective that compares in one sentence and an adverb that compares in the other sentence.

5. _____

_____

6. _____

_____

Changing Final *y* to *i*

Write the Basic Word or Words to answer each question.

1. Which word names big places? _____

2. Which words name living things?

_____, _____,

_____, _____

3. Which words rhyme with lied?

_____, _____,

_____, _____

4. Which word names money you can carry in a pocket?

_____

5. Which verb names what you did when you were late

to something? _____

6. What words make you think of food?

_____, _____

7. Which word names things that you read?

_____

8. Write two words that name something small.

_____, _____

Review   Name a word that is an adjective. _____

Challenge   Write a word that names places. _____

Spelling Words

Basic
1. cities
2. cried
3. puppies
4. hurried
5. stories
6. flies
7. parties
8. tried
9. pennies
10. fried
11. carried
12. babies
13. spied
14. ponies

Review
pretty
very

Challenge
countries
libraries

Name _____ Date _____

Lesson 22
READER'S NOTEBOOK

The Journey: Stories
of Migration
Vocabulary Strategies:
Word Roots

Word Roots

Read each question. Write the word root or word roots in
each underlined word. Then use the underlined word to write
a complete sentence to answer each question.

1. How do grasshoppers <u>survive</u> when there is not enough food?

_____

_____

2. What happens when grasshoppers <u>transform</u> into locusts?

_____

_____

3. Why are locusts so <u>destructive</u> to people's gardens?

_____

_____

4. How do locusts affect <u>transportation</u>?

_____

_____

5. When do gray whales start to look for <u>companions</u>?

_____

_____

6. What do the bodies of the gray whales <u>demand</u> before
   the whales migrate south?

_____

_____

Name _____ Date _____

Lesson 22
READER'S NOTEBOOK

The Journey:
Stories of Migration
Grammar:
Spiral Review

Adjectives and Articles

- The words *a*, *an*, and *the* are special adjectives called **articles**. Use *a* and *an* with singular nouns. Use *a* before words that begin with a consonant sound. Use *an* before words that begin with a vowel sound. Use *the* before both singular and plural nouns.

- An adjective formed from a proper noun should begin with a capital letter.

  <u>The</u> class took <u>a</u> bus to see <u>an</u> exhibit of <u>African</u> zebras.

Rewrite each sentence correctly. Capitalize proper adjectives.

1. We also saw european deer.

_____

2. A irish scientist gave a talk.

_____

Use proofreading marks to write *a*, *an*, and *the* correctly.

Dear Diary,

  We took a trip to see butterflies. We also saw a ant as big as a spider. An guide told us about butterflies in Mexico. He described the stages of an butterfly's life. I asked him an question, and he answered it.

                                Ken

Proofreading for Spelling

Find and circle the misspelled words.

While helping Ms. Mancia in the library, I have spyed many interesting things. I made a list of some of them.

- Two pennys were found in a book about banking!
- Once a man carryed three babies in at one time. He held all three while he looked something up on the computer. Then he hurreed out.
- Two flys landed on a book titled *Insect Homes*.
- A girl cried as she looked at pictures of puppyes.
- A cookbook showed fryed chicken for Valentine's Day. Chicken on Valentine's Day?
- The title of one book was *Farm Storys from Our Big Cityes*.
- Two ponies tryd to climb in through a window. (Okay, I made that one up!)

Spelling Words

Basic
1. cities
2. cried
3. puppies
4. hurried
5. stories
6. flies
7. parties
8. tried
9. pennies
10. fried
11. carried
12. babies
13. spied
14. ponies

Review
pretty
very

Challenge
countries
libraries

Write the misspelled words correctly on the lines below.

1. _____   6. _____

2. _____   7. _____

3. _____   8. _____

4. _____   9. _____

5. _____   10. _____

Connect to Writing

You can make your descriptions clearer by using adjectives and adverbs that compare. To compare two nouns or actions, add -er to most adjectives and adverbs. To compare more than two nouns or actions, add -est to most adjectives and adverbs.

Adjective	Adverb
The blue fish is big.	Dad eats fast.
The white fish is bigger than the blue fish.	My sister eats faster than Dad.
The gray fish is the biggest fish in the tank.	Mom eats the fastest in the family.

**Use the correct form of the adjective or adverb in parentheses.
Write the sentence.**

1. This aquarium is (new) than the one in Tarpon.

_____

2. Tony got to the aquarium (late) than Katie.

_____

3. The jellyfish tank was the (dark) tank in the aquarium.

_____

4. Katie stayed at the seahorse display (long) than at the other displays.

_____

_____

Name _____ Date _____

Lesson 23
READER'S NOTEBOOK

The Journey of
Oliver K. Woodman
Phonics: Suffixes
-ful, -y, -ous, -ly, -er

Suffixes -*ful*, -*y*, -*ous*, -*ly*, -*er*

Read each sentence. Choose the missing word from the box.
Write the word. Then reread the complete sentence.

spoonful	messy	gardener
runner	closely	windy
nervous	bravely	
graceful	joyous	

1. On a _____ day, I have to hold onto my hat!

2. The first _____ of soup is the hottest.

3. The _____ dancer leaped across the stage.

4. Damian _____ walked across the swinging bridge.

5. The _____ planted flowers that would attract bees and butterflies.

6. The lamb followed _____ behind its mother so it wouldn't get lost.

7. My _____ dog spilled her food and tracked mud across the floor.

8. It was a _____ occasion at my house when I brought home a good report card.

9. Do you feel _____ about singing the solo in the school play?

10. When the _____ crossed the finish line, she held her hands over her head in celebration.

Lesson 23
READER'S NOTEBOOK

**The Journey of
Oliver K. Woodman**
Grammar:
Possessive Nouns and Pronouns

Name _____ Date _____

Singular Possessive Nouns

- A **singular possessive noun** shows that a person, animal, place, or thing has or owns something.
- Add an *apostrophe* and *s* to form a singular possessive noun.

  The backpack's straps were loose.

  Oliver's backpack was once home to a mouse.

Thinking Question
Which noun owns or has something?

Write the possessive for each noun below.

1. friend _____

2. Emma _____

3. bus station _____

4. river _____

5. Florida _____

6. car _____

Underline the noun that should be possessive and write the possessive form.

7. The man hobby was to build furniture.   _____

8. The workshop tools hung neatly on the wall.   _____

9. His niece birthday was next week.   _____

10. The day chores would have to wait until
    he completed the gift.   _____

Plural Possessive Nouns

- To form a **plural possessive noun**, add an *apostrophe* to the end of plural nouns that end in *s*.
- Add an *apostrophe* and *s* to the end of plural nouns that do not end in *s*.

Raymond put the sisters' postcards in the mail.

The children's letters were from all over the country.

Thinking Question
Which noun owns or has something?

Write the possessive form of the plural nouns.

1. men _____

2. babies _____

3. books _____

4. fish _____

5. shelves _____

Write sentences for three of the possessive plural nouns.

6. _____

7. _____

8. _____

Spelling Word Sort

Write each Basic Word under the correct heading.

Words that End with the Suffix -*ful*	Words that End with the Suffix -*ly*
_____	_____
_____	_____
_____	_____
_____	_____
_____	_____
_____	_____

Words that End with the Suffix -*er*	
_____	_____
_____	_____
_____	_____

Spelling Words

Basic
1. singer
2. loudly
3. joyful
4. teacher
5. fighter
6. closely
7. powerful
8. farmer
9. quickly
10. careful
11. friendly
12. speaker
13. wonderful
14. truly

Review
hopeful
safely

Challenge
listener
calmly

Review: Add the Review Words to your Word Sort.

Challenge: Add the Challenge Words to your Word Sort.

Focus Trait: Development
Showing Characters' Feelings

Instead of this...	*...a writer wrote this to show feelings.*
Wendy is a good friend.	Wendy is lots of fun to spend a Saturday afternoon with!

A. Read the sentence. Rewrite the sentence to show feelings.

Instead of this...	*...the author wrote this to show feelings.*
1. I liked the food.	

B. Read each event below from *The Journey of Oliver K. Woodman*. Look at the pictures on the pages listed below. Write a line of dialogue in which Oliver shows how he might have felt.

Pair/Share   Work with a partner to brainstorm words that show feelings.

Event	Dialogue with Feelings
2. Oliver rides with three sisters. (pp. 288–289)	
3. Oliver gets to Tameka's house. (pp. 292–293)	

Name _____ Date _____

Cumulative Review

**Read each sentence. Choose the missing word from the box.
Write the word. Then reread the complete sentence.**

salty	handful	numerous
juicy	baker	happily
beautiful	butcher	
finely	dangerous	

1. There are _____ kinds of snacks, and there are many healthful ones to choose from.

2. A _____ of raisins is a good snack. You can grab them and go!

3. Some people like _____ snacks like pretzels or nuts.

4. A _____ can make muffins and breads.

5. Not only do bakeries smell good but the items are _____ to look at.

6. _____ sliced cheese goes well with crackers.

7. There is nothing like a _____ orange as a snack. You can eat it or squeeze it into a glass and drink it.

8. A knife is a _____ tool. The sharp edge could cut a child's fingers.

9. A _____ is trained in using very sharp knives to cut meat.

10. After your snack, smile and go _____ on with your day!

Name _____ Date _____

Lesson 23
READER'S NOTEBOOK

The Journey of
Oliver K. Woodman
Independent Reading

Reader's Guide

The Journey of Oliver K. Woodman

A Timeline of Oliver's Journey

Oliver K. Woodman spent two months traveling from Uncle Ray's house to Tameka's house. First, use details from the text and illustrations to gather information. Then show Oliver's journey on a timeline.

Read pages 274–278. According to Uncle Ray's second letter, when did Oliver K. Woodman begin his journey? Where did he start?

_____

_____

Read pages 279–280. When did Uncle Ray get news of Oliver again? Where was he?

_____

Read page 281. When did Uncle Ray next hear about Oliver? Where was Oliver at that time?

_____

_____

Read page 282. When did Uncle Ray get news next? Where was Oliver?

_____

_____

Read pages 286–287. Uncle Ray and Tameka thought Oliver was lost. When did Uncle Ray get news from Oliver? Where was Oliver?

_____

_____

Read pages 288–289. Where did Oliver end up next? When?

_____

_____

Now use the details that you have gathered to complete the timeline below. Remember to use all the dates from the letters to Uncle Ray that told when Oliver was in each place.

Date

Places

Name _____ Date _____

Lesson 23
READER'S NOTEBOOK

The Journey of Oliver K. Woodman
Grammar:
Possessive Nouns and Pronouns

Possessive Pronouns

Read the sentences below. Underline the possessive pronouns.
If the possessive pronoun is not written correctly, write the word
correctly on the line.

1. Lucy, a friend of our's, is traveling with us to Tennessee.

_____

2. Is this his's map?

_____

3. My favorite part of a road trip is the snacks.

_____

4. That is hers backpack.

_____

5. Is this yours sandwich?

_____

Write a sentence for each of the possessive pronouns.

6. their

_____

7. our

_____

8. my

_____

Suffixes *-ful*, *-ly*, and *-er*

Write a Basic Word to complete each sentence.

1. A person singing in a choir is a _____.

2. If your friends yell during a game, they are playing
   _____.

3. A person who grows corn in the country is a
   _____.

4. If you run fast, you are moving _____.

5. If you are very happy, you are _____.

6. The person whose desk is in the front of your classroom
   is your _____.

7. Someone who is very strong is _____.

8. When you use scissors, you should be _____.

9. A person who smiles and asks you how you are feeling
   is _____.

10. If you are _____ sorry, you will make a
    sincere apology.

Review: Choose a Review Word that completes the sentence.

If you want something to happen, you are _____.

Challenge: Choose a Challenge Word. Use it in a sentence.

_____

Spelling Words
Basic
1. singer
2. loudly
3. joyful
4. teacher
5. fighter
6. closely
7. powerful
8. farmer
9. quickly
10. careful
11. friendly
12. speaker
13. wonderful
14. truly
Review
hopeful
safely
Challenge
listener
calmly

Lesson 23
READER'S NOTEBOOK

**The Journey of
Oliver K. Woodman**
Vocabulary Strategies:
Suffixes -er, -est

Suffixes *-er*, *-est*

**Read the paragraph. Circle the words with the suffix
-er or *-est*. Then write the words the suffixes were added to
on the lines below.**

Saturday was the loveliest, sunniest day we have had
during our car trip. The weather in San Francisco was
colder than I had expected, though. We walked across the
Golden Gate Bridge and met the kindest people. They
were nice to take photos of us. Leaving San Francisco was
harder than leaving Salt Lake City had been, but we were
all happier when we thought about our next adventure.

1. _____	4. _____
2. _____	5. _____
3. _____	6. _____

**Add the suffix *-er* or *-est* to create new words. Complete the
sentence.**

7. nice: Raymond Johnson is the _____ uncle
in the world!

8. dark: The sky is _____ tonight than it was
last night.

9. strange: This is the _____ trip I have ever
taken!

10. young: My sister, Lucinda, is two years _____
than I am.

Name _____ Date _____

Lesson 23
READER'S NOTEBOOK

The Journey of
Oliver K. Woodman
Grammar:
Spiral Review

The Special Verb *be*

- The verbs *am, is, are, was,* and *were* are forms of the verb *be.* They do not show action. They tell what someone or something is or was. *Am, is,* and *are* show present tense. *Was* and *were* show past tense.

  The trip <u>is</u> fun.   The trip <u>was</u> fun.

Write the verb. Write *present* or *past* for each verb.

1. The boys are tired of traveling. _____

2. We were away for one week. _____

3. I am ready to go on another trip. _____

Combine two short sentences by moving one predicate to make one longer sentence with two predicates. Write the new sentence on the line.

4. Father is a good driver. Father is a good storyteller.

_____

5. We are out of the car. We are ready to relax.

_____

6. Mother and Jorge are happy. Mother and Jorge are in the house.

_____

128

Name _____ Date _____

Lesson 23
READER'S NOTEBOOK

The Journey of
Oliver K. Woodman
Spelling:
Suffixes -ful, -ly, and -er

Proofreading for Spelling

Read the following letter. Circle the misspelled words.

Dear Marcus,

My class heard a speeker today. His name was Mr. Brown. He showed us pictures of different parts of the country. We saw a picture of a farmar on his farm. I looked at the picture closelie to see all the animals.

We saw pictures of the Rocky Mountains. What a wunderful trip that would be! I am hopefull that someday I will see the mountains.

Some of my friends were talking lowdley. Mrs. Garcia told them to be quiet. Mrs. Garcia is our teachur.

Mr. Brown answered all of our questions. He was very frenly.

After the speech, we all went kuikly back to our classrooms. I was carefull not to bump into anyone on the way.

Your friend,
Danny

Spelling Words

Basic
1. singer
2. loudly
3. joyful
4. teacher
5. fighter
6. closely
7. powerful
8. farmer
9. quickly
10. careful
11. friendly
12. speaker
13. wonderful
14. truly

Review
hopeful
safely

Challenge
listener
calmly

Write the misspelled words correctly on the lines below.

1. _____   6. _____

2. _____   7. _____

3. _____   8. _____

4. _____   9. _____

5. _____   10. _____

Connect to Writing

You can make your sentences smoother by replacing repeated possessive nouns with possessive pronouns. Make sure the possessive pronoun matches the possessive noun you replace.

Awkward Sentence	Smoother Sentence
My brother's favorite toy is my brother's wooden car.	My brother's favorite toy is his wooden car.
"My cousins' friends are going to my cousins' house," she said.	"My cousins' friends are going to their house," she said.

Replace the underlined possessive noun with a possessive pronoun. Write the sentence.

1. Lucy's favorite aunt is <u>Lucy's</u> Aunt Debra.

   _____

2. The family's first stop will be at the <u>family's</u> old house.

   _____

3. Jack let Lucy borrow <u>Jack's</u> headphones for the trip.

   _____

4. "Will Aunt Debra's new puppy be at <u>Aunt Debra's</u> house?" Lucy asked.

   _____

5. Dad said, "Hand me <u>Dad's</u> car keys."

   _____

Name _____ Date _____

Lesson 24
READER'S NOTEBOOK

Dog-of-the-Sea-Waves
Phonics: Prefixes
un-, pre-, re-, bi-

Prefixes *un-*, *pre-*, *re-*, *bi-*

Read each sentence. Choose the missing word from the box.
Write the word. Then reread the complete sentence.

refilled	preview	unsafe	unbroken
preheat	unopened	biweekly	bicycle
redo	pretest		

1. Did you see the old _____ zoom past?

2. It is _____ to skateboard without a helmet.

3. The _____ showed parts of a new movie.

4. I have to study the words I missed on the spelling

   _____.

5. The _____ magazine comes out every
   two weeks.

6. Mom _____ my glass after I finished the
   first glass of juice.

7. I was happy to find the vase _____ after
   I saw it fall.

8. Tomas had to _____ the poster after he
   misspelled a word on it.

9. I left the gifts _____ while I waited for my
   sisters to come home.

10. The recipe says to _____ the oven to
    325 degrees before putting the chicken in.

Name _____ Date _____

Complex Sentences

- An **independent clause** is a simple sentence and tells a complete thought. It has a subject and a verb.

- A **dependent clause** has a subject and a verb, but it does not tell a complete thought.

- A **complex sentence** is formed by combining one independent clause and one or more dependent clauses.

> Although the boat needed a repair. We went sailing.
>
> Although the boat needed a repair, we went sailing.

Thinking Question
Which part of the sentence tells a complete thought? Which part cannot stand alone?

Write *complex* if the sentence has an independent clause and one or more dependent clauses. Write *dependent clause* if the sentence does not tell a complete thought.

1. When the boat's rope broke, the boys worked quickly to fix it.

   _____

2. Jen retied the ropes since she was good with knots.

   _____

3. While the captain carefully watched her.

   _____

4. Everyone relaxed when they arrived at the dock.

   _____

Name _____ Date _____

Lesson 24
READER'S NOTEBOOK

Dog-of-the-Sea-Waves
Grammar:
Complex Sentences

Subordinating Conjunctions

- A complex sentence is formed by combining one independent clause and at least one dependent clause. If the dependent clause appears first, add a comma after it.

- **Subordinating conjunctions** begin dependent clauses. Some subordinating conjunctions are *after, although, because, before, even though, since, unless, until, when, while.*

  We had fun swimming. Because of the weather.

  We had fun swimming because of the weather.

Thinking Question
Which subordinating conjunction can join the dependent clause to the independent clause?

Underline the dependent clause. Write the subordinating conjunction that begins the dependent clause.

1. We will see the dolphins before we leave.

   _____

2. After we eat lunch, we will see more of the zoo.

   _____

3. Because he forgot his lunch, we went back to the car.

   _____

4. We will miss the dolphins unless we hurry.

   _____

Name _____ Date _____

Spelling Word Sort

Dog-of-the-Sea-Waves
Spelling:
Prefixes *re-*, *un-*

Write each Basic Word under the correct heading.

Prefix that means "again"	Prefix that means "not" or "opposite of"

Spelling Words

Basic
1. unfold
2. rejoin
3. untie
4. reheat
5. unfair
6. unclear
7. repaid
8. rewrite
9. unhurt
10. recheck
11. unlucky
12. unwrap
13. reuse
14. unsure

Review
reread
unsafe

Challenge
unbuckle
unknown

Review: Add the Review Words to your Word Sort.

Challenge: Add the Challenge Words to your Word Sort.

Focus Trait: Elaboration
Using Vivid Details

Good story writers use vivid details to paint a clear picture. Compare the sentence without vivid details to the one with vivid details.

Without Vivid Details: The beach was beautiful in the morning.

With Vivid Details: The sunrise cast a warm glow over the golden sands of the empty beach.

Rewrite each sentence, adding vivid details. You may use ideas from the box below or think of your own.

gently	sparkling	shady	cool

1. They had to cross the ocean to get home.

_____

2. Manu cleaned the animal's wound.

_____

3. He built a shelter from the sun.

_____

4. He gathered berries.

_____

5. He dived into the water.

_____

Cumulative Review

Read each sentence. Choose the missing word from the box. Write the word.

bimonthly	revisit	unequal	rebuild
reelected	preheat	unfriendly	unknown

1. I had so much fun at the park that I hope we _____ it next summer.

2. I asked Uncle Ramon to pour more water into my glass because the amounts in the two glasses were _____.

3. Be sure to _____ the oven before you put the biscuits in to bake.

4. The mayor was _____ for a second term after all the votes were counted.

5. The _____ school newspaper comes out on the first and fifteenth of the month.

6. The _____ store clerk did not look up when I said hello.

7. There was no card on the flowers that were sent by an _____ person.

8. The carpenter had to _____ the wobbly bookshelves.

Reader's Guide

Dog-of-the-Sea-Waves

Homes for Sale!

When the brothers returned home to the southern
sea, they wanted to convince other people to move there.
They decided to place an advertisement in the newspaper.

**Read page 315. What are some details on this page that
will convince people to move to the Hawaiian Islands?**

_____

_____

_____

_____

**Read pages 318–319. Here, Manu finds the hurt seal.
How can the story of the seal help convince people to
move to the islands?**

_____

_____

**Read pages 320–321. On these pages, the brothers were
gathering food. What kinds of food did they gather? Do
you think these details can help convince other people
that Hawaii is a good place to live?**

_____

_____

Now make the advertisement! Show why Hawaii will be a good place to live. The illustration should show the thing you think people would like best about Hawaii. Label the illustration and use details you gathered to write a caption about Hawaii.

_____

_____

_____

_____

Name _____ Date _____

Lesson 24
READER'S NOTEBOOK

Dog-of-the-Sea-Waves
Grammar:
Complex Sentences

Forming Complex Sentences

Combine the clauses to form complex sentences.

1. Even though he is a dog. Rover is Lucy's best friend.

_____

2. She takes Rover to the park. After she comes home from school.

_____

3. Lucy worried she would be late. Unless she hurried.

_____

4. They stayed at the park. Until it started to rain.

_____

5. Because it was raining. They ran to the house.

_____

6. When they got home. Rover shook water everywhere.

_____

Dog-of-the-Sea-Waves
Spelling:
Prefixes *re-*, *un-*

Prefixes *re-*, *un-*

Write a Basic Word to answer each clue.

1. You might do this with shoelaces. _____

2. You would do this to a present wrapped in paper.

   _____

3. You might feel this way if you didn't know the answer to

   a question. _____

4. To be sure your answers on a test were correct, you

   might do this. _____

5. If you thought someone had cheated in a game, you

   might think the game was this. _____

6. You could do this to make some leftover food warm

   again. _____

7. If you didn't like a poem you had written, you might do

   this to it. _____

8. You would do this to a shirt you found folded in a

   drawer. _____

Review: Choose a Review Word. Write a clue for it.

_____

Challenge: Choose a Challenge Word. Write a clue for it.

_____

Spelling Words

Basic
1. unfold
2. rejoin
3. untie
4. reheat
5. unfair
6. unclear
7. repaid
8. rewrite
9. unhurt
10. recheck
11. unlucky
12. unwrap
13. reuse
14. unsure

Review
reread
unsafe

Challenge
unbuckle
unknown

Name _____ Date _____

Shades of Meaning

Read each sentence. Choose the word from the box that best completes each sentence. Explain your choice.

knows	suspects	wonders	believes	hears
know	suspect	wonder	believe	hear

1. How does Hoku _____ that the star he

discovered always points north?

_____

_____

2. As the brothers sail away from the island, Opua

_____ whether he sees smoke or a cloud.

_____

_____

3. For a while, the brothers _____ that Manu

has drowned in the sea.

_____

_____

4. Although they are leaving the island, Manu

_____ that he and his brothers will return.

_____

_____

Name _____ Date _____

Lesson 24
READER'S NOTEBOOK

Dog-of-the-Sea-Waves
Grammar:
Spiral Review

Possessive Nouns and Pronouns

- A possessive noun shows that a person, place, or thing has or owns something.
- Add an apostrophe and *s* to a singular noun to make it possessive. Add an apostrophe to a plural noun that ends in *s*.
- Possessive pronouns can take the place of possessive nouns. Possessive pronouns show ownership: *my, your, his, her, its, our, their.*

  The <u>family's</u> outing was to the zoo.
  The <u>seals'</u> pool was new.
  <u>Their</u> bodies moved quickly through the water.

Use the correct possessive form of the noun in parentheses to complete each sentence.

1. It was _____ first visit to the zoo. (Charlie)
2. The _____ Australia section has koalas. (zoo)
3. The _____ uniforms are a dark green. (workers)

Use a possessive pronoun to take the place of the underlined possessive noun. Write the sentence.

4. Yolanda saw the dolphin's head peek out of the water.

_____

5. The dolphin splashed water onto Yolanda's shoes.

_____

Proofreading for Spelling

Dog-of-the-Sea-Waves
Spelling:
Prefixes *re-*, *un-*

Read each direction. Circle the misspelled words.

1. Set up your tent.
First, unfolde the tent.

2. Next, unrap the tent ropes. You need the ropes to set up your tent.

3. If ropes are tied, you need to untye them.

4. Try to reus plastic bags while at camp. Do not throw them away.

5. Do not reheet drinks or food. See your camp leader.

6. Be sure to rejoyn your group after lunch.

7. Always walk with a friend. Walking alone at camp is unsaff.

8. Are you sure you have everything? You should rechek your bag.

Spelling Words

1. unfold
2. rejoin
3. untie
4. reheat
5. unfair
6. unclear
7. repaid
8. rewrite
9. unhurt
10. recheck
11. unlucky
12. unwrap
13. reuse
14. unsure

Review
reread
unsafe

Challenge
unbuckle
unknown

Write the misspelled words correctly on the lines below.

1. _____   5. _____

2. _____   6. _____

3. _____   7. _____

4. _____   8. _____

Connect to Writing

Short, choppy sentences can be combined to make your writing smoother. Use a subordinating conjunction to form complex sentences. Remember to use a comma after the dependent clause if it comes first in the sentence.

Short Sentences	Longer, Smoother Sentences
Sam taught his cat. He thought the cat was clever.	Sam taught his cat since he thought the cat was clever.
Dave played with his pet. He was happy.	While Dave played with his pet, he was happy.

Use a subordinating conjunction from the word bank to combine two short, choppy sentences. Write the new sentence on the line.

Word Bank

since   while   though   because

1. Tara's dog swims with her. It is not fond of water.

_____

2. Ernesto worked with his bird. He waited for his friend.

_____

3. His bird escapes often. It knows how to open its cage.

_____

4. Bennie's cat is still healing. It needs to wear a bandage.

_____

Name _____ Date _____

Lesson 25
READER'S NOTEBOOK

Mountains: Surviving on
Mt. Everest
Phonics:
Suffixes -less, -ness, -able

Suffixes -less, -ness, -able

Read each sentence. Choose the missing word from
the box. Write the word. Then reread the complete sentence.

boneless	predictable	enjoyable	happiness
painless	weightless	shyness	softness
breakable	darkness		

1. Patricia got over her _____ when she met the new neighors'
   puppy.

2. That story was so _____ that I guessed the ending.

3. The newborn chicks are so light that they almost feel _____.

4. I needed a flashlight to see in the _____.

5. Since I didn't need a shot, my doctor's visit was _____.

6. Chris smiled and clapped at the end of the _____ movie.

7. Be careful not to drop the box because it contains _____
   items.

8. Mr. Griffin said, "The children in my classroom have brought me much

   joy and _____."

9. When you eat _____ chicken there are no bones left on
   the plate!

10. Bradley sank back into the _____ of the pillow.

Adjectives That Compare

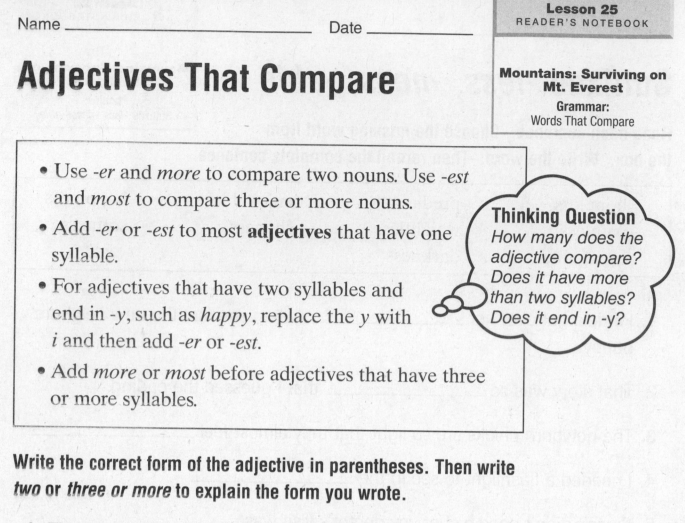

- Use -er and *more* to compare two nouns. Use -*est* and *most* to compare three or more nouns.
- Add -er or -*est* to most **adjectives** that have one syllable.
- For adjectives that have two syllables and end in -*y*, such as *happy*, replace the *y* with *i* and then add -er or -*est*.
- Add *more* or *most* before adjectives that have three or more syllables.

Thinking Question
How many does the adjective compare? Does it have more than two syllables? Does it end in -y?

Write the correct form of the adjective in parentheses. Then write *two* **or** *three or more* **to explain the form you wrote.**

1. This backpack is (light) than that one. _____

2. I think that mountain climbing is (dangerous) than hiking trails. _____

3. The winds on this mountain are the (powerful) I have ever experienced. _____

4. The trail going up was (uneven) than the trail coming down. _____

5. Our pack mule was the (noisy) animal on the trail. _____

Name _____ Date _____

Lesson 25
READER'S NOTEBOOK

Mountains: Surviving on
Mt. Everest
Grammar:
Words That Compare

Adverbs That Compare

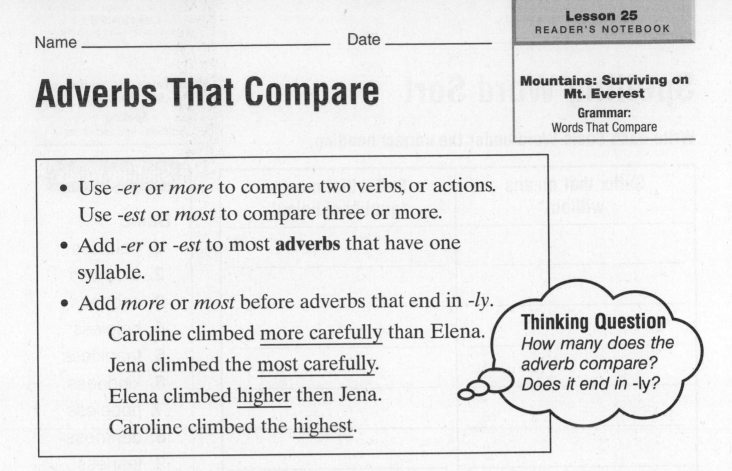

- Use *-er* or *more* to compare two verbs, or actions.
  Use *-est* or *most* to compare three or more.
- Add *-er* or *-est* to most **adverbs** that have one syllable.
- Add *more* or *most* before adverbs that end in *-ly*.
  Caroline climbed <u>more carefully</u> than Elena.
  Jena climbed the <u>most carefully</u>.
  Elena climbed <u>higher</u> then Jena.
  Caroline climbed the <u>highest</u>.

Thinking Question
How many does the adverb compare? Does it end in -ly?

Write the correct form of the adverb in parentheses. Then write
two or *three or more* **to explain the form you wrote.**

1. Will waited (patiently) than Kyle for the storm to pass.

   _____

2. Kyle handled the ropes for the tent (roughly) of all
   the climbers.

   _____

3. The ropes were tied (tight) by the oldest climber.

   _____

4. The climbers sitting by the fire felt (warm) than those
   inside the tent.

   _____

5. Will slept (quietly) of all the campers.

   _____

Spelling Word Sort

Mountains: Surviving on Mt. Everest

Spelling:
Suffixes -*less* and -*ness*

Write each Basic Word under the correct heading.

Suffix that means "without"	Suffix that means "quality of being"
_____	_____
_____	_____
_____	_____
_____	_____
_____	_____
_____	_____
_____	_____
_____	_____
_____	_____
_____	_____

Challenge: Add the Challenge Words to your Word Sort.

Spelling Words

Basic
1. painless
2. sickness
3. sadness
4. helpless
5. thankless
6. kindness
7. hopeless
8. darkness
9. fearless
10. thickness
11. careless
12. goodness
13. spotless
14. softness

Review
useful
weakly

Challenge
breathless
eagerness

Name _____ Date _____

Lesson 25
READER'S NOTEBOOK

Mountains: Surviving on
Mt. Everest
Writing:
Narrative Writing

Focus Trait: Coventions
Misspelled Words

As writers complete the final drafts, they proofread their writing to make sure they have spelled each word correctly.

Find the misspelled word or words in each sentence. Then rewrite the sentence with the words spelled correctly.

1. Mt. Everest is a towering mountin.

   _____

2. Temba made a terrible mistak and took off his gloves

   _____

3. After nightfall, the temprature plungd.

   _____

4. Temba fought to reach the summet.

   _____

5. Climers must be wary of huge peices of ice that could crush them.

   _____

Name _____ Date _____

Lesson 25
READER'S NOTEBOOK

Mountains: Surviving on
Mt. Everest
Phonics:
Cumulative Review

Cumulative Review

Read each sentence. Choose the missing word from
the box. Write the word. Then reread the complete
sentence.

redo	sleepless	freshness	crispness
preview	erasable	tasteless	valuable

1. Justin spent a _____ night at the campout because he was
worried about bears.

2. To test the _____ of celery, see if it makes a snapping sound.

3. The painting is _____ because it is one of a kind.

4. After one sip of the _____ soup, Tessa switched and ate
something with more flavor.

5. I like to draw in pencil because it is _____, and I can fix
my mistakes.

6. Daniel always smells each melon to test its _____ before
buying it.

7. I made so many mistakes, I had to _____ the whole
assignment.

8. We got to _____ the movie before it came to the local theater.

Name _____ Date _____

Lesson 25
READER'S NOTEBOOK

Mountains: Surviving
on Mt. Everest
Independent Reading

Reader's Guide

Mountains: Surviving on Mt. Everest

Create a Travel Brochure

You are writing a travel brochure about climbing
Mount Everest. First, gather details for the brochure.

**Read pages 349 and 351. Write important details
about Mount Everest and its mountain range.**

_____

_____

_____

Read page 354. What equipment should travelers bring?

_____

_____

_____

**Read pages 355 and 360. What should travelers know about the
climb? What should they be careful *not* to do?**

_____

_____

_____

Name _____ Date _____

Lesson 25
READER'S NOTEBOOK

Mountains: Surviving
on Mt. Everest
Independent Reading

Now use all the details from the previous page to
write a brochure that will tell climbers what to
expect on Mount Everest and what to bring for the climb.
Include a title and labeled illustrations on each panel of
the brochure to show what that section talks about.

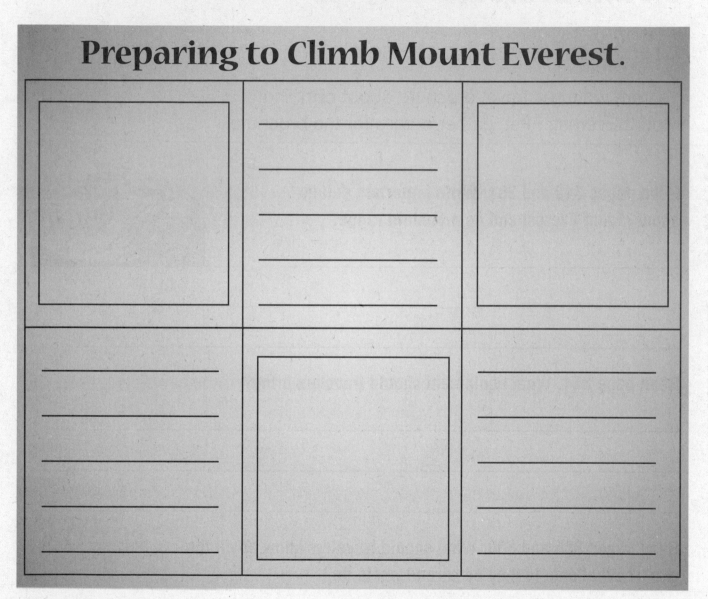

Name _____ Date _____

Lesson 25
READER'S NOTEBOOK

Mountains: Surviving on Mt. Everest
Grammar:
Words That Compare

Adjectives and Adverbs That Compare

**Write an adjective or adverb to complete each sentence.
Then write *adjective* or *adverb* to tell about the word or phrase
you used.**

1. Jeff explained the day's events _____ than
   Ella. (calm) _____

2. The water at the bottom of the stream was
   _____ than the water on the surface.
   (murky) _____

3. Laurie was the _____ worker of them all.
   (fast) _____

4. Jason had the _____ sneakers in the group.
   (muddy) _____

**Write two sentences. Include an adjective that compares in one
sentence and an adverb that compares in the other sentence.**

5. _____

   _____

6. _____

   _____

153

Name _____ Date _____

Lesson 25
READER'S NOTEBOOK

Suffixes -*less* and -*ness*

Mountains: Surviving on Mt. Everest
Spelling:
Suffixes -*less* and -*ness*

Write the Basic Word that makes sense in the sentence.

1. The hiker thanked the guide for her help and
   _____.

2. In high mountains, a lack of oxygen can cause

   _____

3. Being _____ in the mountains is
   dangerous.

4. It is not wise to climb mountains in

   _____.

5. The _____ guide climbed the
   high cliff.

6. I was amazed at the _____ of the
   freshly fallen snow.

7. Scientists measured the _____ of
   the ice at the top.

Challenge: Choose a Challenge Word. Use it in a sentence.

_____

_____

Spelling Words

Basic
1. painless
2. sickness
3. sadness
4. helpless
5. thankless
6. kindness
7. hopeless
8. darkness
9. fearless
10. thickness
11. careless
12. goodness
13. spotless
14. softness

Review
useful
weakly

Challenge
breathless
eagerness

Lesson 25
READER'S NOTEBOOK

Mountains: Surviving on
Mt. Everest
Vocabulary Strategies:
Analogies

Analogies

Complete the analogies with a word from the box.

danger	increase	assist	departure
succeed	brave	slope	strength

1. <u>Believable</u> is to <u>unbelievable</u> as <u>weakness</u> is to _____.

2. <u>Force</u> is to <u>power</u> as <u>achieve</u> is to _____.

3. <u>Polite</u> is to <u>rude</u> as <u>fearful</u> is to _____.

4. <u>Excellent</u> is to <u>wonderful</u> as <u>risk</u> is to _____.

5. <u>Frequent</u> is to <u>often</u> as <u>aid</u> is to _____.

6. <u>Up</u> is to <u>down</u> as <u>arrival</u> is to _____.

7. <u>Sad</u> is to <u>happy</u> as <u>decrease</u> is to _____.

8. <u>Ocean</u> is to <u>wave</u> as <u>mountain</u> is to _____.

Name _____ Date _____

Lesson 25
READER'S NOTEBOOK

Mountains: Surviving on
Mt. Everest
Grammar:
Spiral Review

Forming Complex Sentences

> • A **complex sentence** is formed by combining one independent clause and one or more dependent clauses. If the dependent clause appears first, add a comma after it.
>
> • **Subordinating conjunctions** begin dependent clauses. Some subordinating clauses are: *after, although, because, before, even though, since, unless, until, when, while.*

Combine the clauses to form complex sentences.

1. Even though he was tired. Tracy hiked up the hill.

   _____

2. Torry planned to climb the hill. When her father could join her.

   _____

3. Because she is afraid of heights. Rita will not climb.

   _____

4. Until he saw the hill. Robbie was eager to climb.

   _____

5. They played catch. While they waited for the others to climb.

   _____

6. Mel climbed again. Before they went home.

   _____

Proofreading for Spelling

Read each journal entry. Circle the misspelled words.

Journal of a Mountain Guide

Monday: We rescued a hiker who had become lost in the darkniss.

Tuesday: It is hopless to teach some people how to be careful in the mountains. They just don't pay attention.

Wednesday: We took a short hike to the ranger station. It was paneless.

Thursday: Felt a strange thikness in my leg. I'll have a doctor check it tomorrow. Was glad for the softnes of my sleeping bag.

Friday: Found a hammer and some rope in the snow. Some careluss hiker must have dropped them.

Saturday: Some hikers thanked us for our kineness. I guess being a mountain guide is not always a thankliss job!

Spelling Words

Basic
1. painless
2. sickness
3. sadness
4. helpless
5. thankless
6. kindness
7. hopeless
8. darkness
9. fearless
10. thickness
11. careless
12. goodness
13. spotless
14. softness

Review
useful
weakly

Challenge
breathless
eagerness

Write the misspelled words correctly on the lines below.

1. _____   5. _____

2. _____   6. _____

3. _____   7. _____

4. _____   8. _____

Name _____ Date _____

Lesson 25
READER'S NOTEBOOK

Mountains: Surviving on Mt. Everest
Grammar:
Connect to Writing

Connect to Writing

Use adjectives and adverbs that compare to make your ideas easier for readers to picture. To compare two nouns or actions, add *-er* to most adjectives and adverbs. To compare more than two nouns or actions, add *-est* to most adjectives and adverbs. Use *more* or *most* before an adverb that ends in *-ly*.

	Compare Two	**Compare More Than Two**
Adjective	Molly's backpack is heavier than Jeff's.	Steven has the heaviest backpack of everyone in the class.
Adverb	Stacy climbs more easily than Brett.	Mike climbs most easily of everyone in the group.

Choose the correct form of the adjective or adverb in parentheses. Write the sentence.

1. Mrs. Brown's map is (newer, newest) than my map.

   _____

2. Where are the (higher, highest) mountains in the world?

   _____

3. Brynn spoke (more eagerly, most eagerly) about climbing than Jo.

   _____

4. Of all the climbers, Lucas climbed (more powerfully, most powerfully).

   _____

Name _____ Date _____

Lesson 26
READER'S NOTEBOOK

**The Foot Race
Across America**
Phonics: Common Final
Syllables -tion, -sion, -ture

Common Final Syllables

**Choose a word from the box to complete each sentence.
Read the completed sentence.**

Word Bank				
action	attention	confusion	discussion	furniture
future	motion	nature	picture	protection

1. Give me the camera and I will take your _____ .

2. No one knew what to do, so there was a lot of _____ .

3. If you push the toy car, you set it in _____ .

4. This is important news, so pay _____ .

5. Yesterday is the past, and tomorrow is the _____ .

6. An umbrella gives you _____ from the rain.

7. Let's have a _____ to talk about our plans.

8. Tables, chairs, and sofas are kinds of _____ .

9. I like that pirate movie because it has lots of _____ .

10. Trees, animals, and clouds are all parts of _____ .

Reader's Guide

The Foot Race Across America

Write a Speech

Andy Payne is receiving an award after the race, but first he must give a speech. Note important details from the text before you write the speech.

Read page 7. What were the specific details of the race that Andy saw in the newspaper?

_____

_____

Why did Andy want to run in the race?

_____

_____

Read pages 8–9. What was the first part of the race like?

_____

_____

Read page 10. What troubles did Andy and the runners face?

_____

_____

Read pages 12–14. What happened at the end of the race?

_____

_____

Name _____ Date _____

The announcer steps onto the stage and says,
"We will now present the award for Greatest Running
Achievement to Andy Payne. Andy, please tell us about
the race!" Write Andy's speech.

_____

_____

_____

_____

_____

_____

_____

_____

_____

_____

_____

_____

_____

_____

_____

_____

Lesson 26
READER'S NOTEBOOK

The Foot Race Across America
Spelling: Words with VCCV Pattern

Words with the VCCV Pattern

Basic: Write the Basic Word that best fits each clue.

1. get pleasure from

2. an error

3. a human being

4. where flowers grow

5. opposite of *remember*

6. a baseball official

7. a command

8. protects your head

9. opposite of *solution*

10. soft floor covering

1. _____

2. _____

3. _____

4. _____

5. _____

6. _____

7. _____

8. _____

9. _____

10. _____

Spelling Words

Basic
1. person
2. helmet
3. until
4. carpet
5. Monday
6. enjoy
7. forget
8. problem
9. Sunday
10. garden
11. order
12. mistake
13. umpire
14. herself

Challenge
expect
wisdom

Challenge: Write two sentences about how you might help a friend reach a goal. Use both of the Challenge Words.

_____

_____

_____

Lesson 26
READER'S NOTEBOOK

The Foot Race
Across America
Spelling: Words with VCCV
Pattern

Name _____ Date _____

Word Sort

Write each Basic Word next to the correct heading.

Vowel *a* in first syllable	
Vowel *e* in first syllable	
Vowel *i* in first syllable	
Vowel *o* in first syllable	
Vowel *u* in first syllable	

Challenge: Add the Challenge Words to your Word Sort.

Spelling Words

Basic
1. person
2. helmet
3. until
4. carpet
5. Monday
6. enjoy
7. forget
8. problem
9. Sunday
10. garden
11. order
12. mistake
13. umpire
14. herself

Challenge
expect
wisdom

Proofreading for Spelling

**Find the misspelled words and circle them. Write them
correctly on the numbered lines below.**

Some Really Super Softball!

Last Sundy, the Braden Bobcats' fans got a big thrill
when the Bobcats beat the Pinehill Pumas.

The game was tied 1–1 in the last inning. The Bobcat
batters came up in ordor. First came Polly Peters, who
looked ready to win that game all by herrself. The Puma
pitcher, though, couldn't find the plate, and the umpeire
called four balls in a row. Polly walked to first base.

The next persen up to bat was Miko Myata. This time,
the Puma pitcher's probblem was wild pitches. When one
pitch hit Miko's helmit, Miko strolled to first base and Polly
moved to second.

The pitcher made one last misteak when he threw a
perfect pitch. Shayla Smith swung mightily. CRACK! That
ball was out of the park, and it probably didn't land untill
Munday. The Bobcats won it, 4–1!

Spelling Words

Basic
1. person
2. helmet
3. until
4. carpet
5. Monday
6. enjoy
7. forget
8. problem
9. Sunday
10. garden
11. order
12. mistake
13. umpire
14. herself

1. _____   6. _____

2. _____   7. _____

3. _____   8. _____

4. _____   9. _____

5. _____   10. _____

Abbreviations for Days and Months

- An **abbreviation** is a shortened form of a word. Most abbreviations begin with a capital letter and end with a period.

  Monday; Mon.

  August; Aug.

Thinking Question
Is the word a day of the week or a month of the year?

Write the correct abbreviation for each day and month.

1. Sunday _____

2. December _____

3. Tuesday _____

4. Thursday _____

5. Saturday _____

6. November _____

7. Wednesday _____

8. September _____

9. Friday _____

10. February _____

Name _____ Date _____

Abbreviations for Places

- An **abbreviation** is a shortened form of a word.
- Places with names that can be abbreviated include roads, streets, lanes, avenues, and boulevards. Examples include *Harrison Rd.*, *Maple St.*, *Elmira Ln.*, *Plainville Ave.*, and *Broad Blvd*.

Thinking Question
Is the word the name of a place?

Write each place name correctly. Use capital letters and abbreviations.

1. King Boulevard _____

2. Jefferson Street _____

3. Western Avenue _____

4. Oak Road _____

5. Chestnut Lane _____

6. Ocean Boulevard _____

7. Washington Street _____

8. Smith Lane _____

9. Vermont Avenue _____

10. Lincoln Street _____

Lesson 26
READER'S NOTEBOOK

**The Foot Race
Across America**
Grammar:
Abbreviations

Writing Abbreviations

1–5. Write the correct abbreviation for each day and month.

1. Tuesday _____

2. January _____

3. Friday _____

4. October _____

5. Saturday _____

6–10. Abbreviate each place name correctly.

6. Myer Lane _____

7. Hudson Street _____

8. Prospect Road _____

9. Lynn Boulevard _____

10. North Avenue _____

Name _____ Date _____

Lesson 26
READER'S NOTEBOOK

**The Foot Race
Across America**
Grammar: Spiral Review

Possessive Nouns

- A **possessive noun** shows that a person, an animal, or a thing owns or has something.
- To show that **one** person, animal, or thing has possession, add an **apostrophe** and -s **('s).**
- To show that **more than one** person, animal, or thing has possession, add an -s and an **apostrophe (s').**

Noun	Singular Possessive Noun	Plural Possessive Noun
teacher	teacher's	teachers'
book	book's	books'

Activity: Write the word in parentheses as a possessive noun to complete the sentence.

1. _____ home is in Oklahoma. (Andy)

2. He runs in his _____ neighborhood. (cousin)

3. Andy likes to run with the _____ children. (neighbors)

4. He times his running with his _____ stopwatch. (sister)

5. The _____ prize is a huge trophy. (winner)

6. The _____ families all watched the race. (runners)

7. Allen could hear the _____ chirps as he ran. (bird)

8. Each _____ shirt had a number. (contestant)

9. Every runner could hear the _____ cheers. (fans)

10. The _____ statue of Andy shows him running. (town)

Name _____ Date _____

Lesson 26
READER'S NOTEBOOK

The Foot Race
Across America
Grammar
Connect to Writing

Conventions: Proofreading

Proofreading your work for correctly spelled **abbreviations** will make your writing stronger.

Incorrect Abbreviation	Correct Abbreviation
tues; mar	Tues.; Mar.
av; rd	Ave.; Rd.

Use proofreading marks to write abbreviations correctly in this informal note.

Sun, Oct 3

Liam,

    We stopped by Pleasant Str on fri and met your uncle's family. He is a wonderful man, and his kids and wife are great, too. We met Pat Smith, who is very nice. He lives in Miami. He has a house on Beach Blvd, near the ocean. We are going to meet him and Cindy Birch next Tues for a clambake.

                    Lucy

Proofreading Marks
¶ Indent
∧ Add
ꝰ Delete
≡ Capital letter
/ Small letter

Focus Trait: Organization

Read each sentence that gives a comparing or contrasting detail. Write whether it compares or contrasts.

_____ Andy Payne and Peter Gavuzzi both competed in the International Trans-Continental Foot Race.

_____ Both men were called "Bunioneers."

_____ Andy was from Oklahoma, while Peter was from England.

_____ Andy won in 1928, but Peter won in 1929.

Think of a topic sentence for a paragraph that compares Andy and Peter. Write the sentence. Then write a topic sentence for a paragraph that contrasts Andy and Peter.

Comparing paragraph:

_____

_____

Contrasting paragraph:

_____

_____

Name _____ Date _____

Lesson 27
READER'S NOTEBOOK

**The Power
of Magnets**
Phonics: Double Consonants

Double Consonants

Choose a syllable from the left box and a syllable from the
right box to make a word that completes each sentence. Write
the word on the line and read the completed sentence.

Hint: Each word you make will have a double consonant.

First Syllables					Second Syllables				
at	but	dol	fun	hap	den	der	lar	low	nel
lad	sud	tun	yel	zip	ny	pen	per	ter	tract

1. A magnet will _____ a needle.

2. What do you think will _____ next in that story?

3. Bonnie needs a _____ marker to color the sun.

4. I spread _____ on warm toast.

5. All of a _____, it started to rain.

6. I can't close my jacket because the _____ is broken.

7. Climb up the _____ carefully.

8. That joke was so _____ that I hurt myself laughing.

9. Jake has one _____ to buy a treat.

10. A mole will dig a _____ under the ground.

Reader's Guide

The Power of Magnets

Your Magnet Invention

Now is your chance to design a magnet to make your
life easier! First, answer the questions below to make
sure you understand how magnets work. Then, create
your own design.

Read pages 20–21. What causes some objects to be attracted to a magnet?

_____

_____

Read page 22. What happens if you sprinkle iron filings around a magnet?

_____

_____

Read page 23. What is important about electromagnets?

_____

_____

Read pages 24–25. How can you create a magnetic field in your own home?

_____

_____

Now think of a way that you can use a magnet to improve your life. Will you use the magnet in your home or outside? Will you use it at school? Will you use a regular magnet or an electromagnet? Draw a picture of your magnet and write an explanation of how it works. Be sure that you include details from the text in your design.

_____

_____

_____

_____

Double Consonants

The Power of Magnets
Spelling: Words with
Double Consonants

Basic: Write the Basic Word that best completes each group.

1. sheet, blanket, _____

2. chapter, unit, _____

3. dime, quarter, _____

4. jam, preserves, _____

5. fox, raccoon, _____

6. top, side, _____

7. postcard, note, _____

8. peach, plum, _____

9. milk, cheese, _____

10. zipper, snap, _____

Spelling Words

Basic

1. jelly
2. bottom
3. pillow
4. happen
5. butter
6. lesson
7. cherry
8. sudden
9. arrow
10. dollar
11. hello
12. rabbit
13. letter
14. button

Challenge

stubborn

mirror

Challenge: Use one of the Challenge Words to write a sentence.

_____

_____

_____

Word Sort

Write each Basic Word next to the correct heading.

Words with three letters in both syllables	_____ _____	
	_____ _____	
	_____ _____	
	_____ _____	
	_____ _____	
	_____ _____	
Words with two letters in one of the two syllables	_____ _____	
	_____ _____	
Words with four letters in both syllables	_____ _____	

Basic
1. jelly
2. bottom
3. pillow
4. happen
5. butter
6. lesson
7. cherry
8. sudden
9. arrow
10. dollar
11. hello
12. rabbit
13. letter
14. button

Challenge
stubborn
mirror

Challenge: Add the Challenge Words to your Word Sort.

Proofreading for Spelling

Find the misspelled words and circle them. Write them correctly on the lines below.

Dear Jamal,

Can you believe you're getting a leter from me, at last? I think of you a lot, especially when I see a jar of that charry jellie you love so much. Mom bought some the other day, and all of a suddin, I find that I love it, too!

One of my front teeth fell out last week. I put the tooth under my pilloaw. The next morning, a doller showed up there. Maybe that's enough to buy a treat for my pet rabit.

Hey, you're a science buff, right? Do you happan to know much about magnets? We had a really neat lessone on them in science class last week, and I'd love to talk to you about them.

Well, say hellow to your family for me. Please write back if you can. I miss you!

Your friend,

Curtis

Spelling Words
1. jelly
2. bottom
3. pillow
4. happen
5. butter
6. lesson
7. cherry
8. sudden
9. arrow
10. dollar
11. hello
12. rabbit
13. letter
14. button

1. _____ 5. _____ 9. _____

2. _____ 6. _____ 10. _____

3. _____ 7. _____

4. _____ 8. _____

Name _____ Date _____

Lesson 27
READER'S NOTEBOOK

The Power of Magnets
Grammar
Contractions

Contractions with *not*

You can put together two words and make a
contraction. An apostrophe (') takes the place of any
letter or letters that are left out. Many contractions
combine a verb with *not*. The contraction *won't* is
special. You form it from the words *will not* and
change the spelling.

Thinking Questions
*Which verb am I
putting together with
the word* not*? Which
letter should I leave
out and replace with
an apostrophe?*

It **is not** *always easy to invent something.*
It **isn't** *always easy to invent something.*

Michael Faraday **was not** *afraid to try something new.*
Michael Faraday **wasn't** *afraid to try something new.*

**Write the contraction for the words in parentheses. Use an
apostrophe in place of the underlined letter or letters.**

1. Electromagnets _____ work unless they are turned on. (do n<u>o</u>t)

2. The magnet in the poem _____ get used anymore. (does n<u>o</u>t)

3. A computer's hard drive _____ work correctly without an

   electromagnet. (will n<u>o</u>t)

4. We _____ aware that doorbells use electromagnets. (were n<u>o</u>t)

5. A blow dryer also _____ work without an electromagnet.

   (would n<u>o</u>t)

6. The poem's speaker _____ been allowed to make her brother

   disappear. (has n<u>o</u>t)

7. I _____ see a magnetic field, but I know it exists. (can<u>no</u>t)

8. I _____ believe all the things magnets do! (could n<u>o</u>t)

Contractions with Pronouns

You can put a pronoun and a verb together to make a contraction. An apostrophe replaces the letter or letters that are left out.

*She says that **she is** working on a project.*
*She says that **she's** working on a project.*

***We will** see if it turns out.*
***We'll** see if it turns out.*

Thinking Question
When I join a pronoun with a verb, which letters should I leave out and replace with an apostrophe to make a contraction?

Write the contraction for the words in parentheses. Use an apostrophe in place of the underlined letter or letters.

1. _____ be exciting to find out if the experiment works. (It w<u>i</u>ll)

2. _____ read a lot about experiments with magnets. (We h<u>a</u>ve)

3. Make sure _____ ready for the science fair. (you <u>a</u>re)

4. _____ going to enter the science fair, too. (I <u>a</u>m)

5. _____ judge whose project is the best. (They w<u>i</u>ll)

6. _____ going to be competitive. (It <u>i</u>s)

7. _____ almost finished our project. (We h<u>a</u>ve)

8. She says _____ enter the science fair next year. (she w<u>i</u>ll)

Contractions

1–5. Write the contraction for the words in parentheses. Use an apostrophe in place of the underlined letter or letters.

1. We _____ gone to the science fair before. (have n<u>o</u>t)

2. My family _____ know how much fun it would be. (did n<u>o</u>t)

3. My sister _____ stop playing with the projects. (would n<u>o</u>t)

4. My brother _____ wait to enter the science fair himself. (can<u>no</u>t)

5. We _____ mind competing against each other. (will n<u>o</u>t)

6–10. Write the contraction for the words in parentheses. Use an apostrophe in place of the underlined letter or letters.

6. _____ going to love the science fair. (You <u>a</u>re)

7. My teacher says _____ won a prize. (I <u>ha</u>ve)

8. _____ give it to me later. (She <u>wi</u>ll)

9. _____ hang in my bedroom. (It <u>wi</u>ll)

10. _____ the best prize I ever won. (It <u>i</u>s)

Writing Proper Nouns

- A **proper noun** always begins with a capital letter.
- Days, months, holidays, historical periods, and special events are proper nouns.
- The first, last, and important words in a book title are capitalized. Book titles are underlined.

Proper Nouns	
day	Wednesday
month	March
holiday	Thanksgiving
book title	The Giver

Activity: Write all proper nouns and book titles from each sentence correctly.

1. The electricity went off last friday. _____

2. I read my favorite book, the dark forest, with a flashlight.

   _____

3. We saved a lot of electricity in april. _____

4. My book report on Michael Faraday is due after memorial

   day. _____

5. I would rather learn about world war II than about

   electricity. _____

6. My sister is writing a book called when the lights go out.

   _____

Conventions: Proofreading

Sentences Without Correct Contractions	Sentences with Correct Contractions
Shes making her project.	She's making her project.
The project is'nt too difficult.	The project isn't too difficult.
We have't decided what we'ill make.	We haven't decided what we'll make.

Proofread the paragraphs. Find and underline five mistakes in the spelling of contractions. Write the correct sentences on the lines below.

Theyr'e starting to organize this year's science fair. I cann't miss it this time! Last year I was'nt able to get a project done in time. This year I'm going to make sure I do.

Iv'e heard the fairs are a lot of fun. You get to see all the projects other people have worked on. I would'nt want to miss that.

1. _____

2. _____

3. _____

4. _____

5. _____

Focus Trait: Elaboration

Read each problem and solution. Add details to elaborate. Explain how the problem was solved and how the solution works. Use information from "The Power of Magnets."

1.   **Problem:** Kaylie dropped a box of pins.
     Solution: She used a magnet.
Details:

_____

_____

2.   **Problem:** The remote control car does not work.
     Solution: We put a battery in it.
Details:

_____

_____

3.   **Problem:** A junkyard owner needs to move a car.
     Solution: He flips a switch.
Details:

_____

_____

4.   **Problem:** Michael Faraday wanted to produce electricity.
     Solution: He moved a magnet through a coil of wire.
Details:

_____

_____

Name _____ Date _____

Words with *ough*, *augh*

**Read each word in the box. Say the sound that *ough* or *augh*
stands for. Then write the word in the chart under the correct
category.**

Word Bank					
bought	caught	fought	naughty	rough	taught
brought	daughter	laugh	ought	sought	thought

ough rhymes with *paw*	*ough* rhymes with *puff*	*augh* rhymes with *paw*	*augh* rhymes with *staff*

Name _____ Date _____

Lesson 28
READER'S NOTEBOOK

Becoming Anything
He Wants to Be
Independent Reading

Reader's Guide

Becoming Anything He Wants to Be

Create a Captioned Illustration

This story of Erik Weihenmayer is told with photographs that have captions. The photographs help us see what Erik can do, and the captions help us understand the photographs. Let's take a closer look.

Look at page 35. What does the caption let you know about the photograph on this page?

_____

_____

Look at page 37. What does the caption tell you about the photograph on this page?

_____

_____

Look at page 38. In the first photograph, which of the bike riders is Erik? How do you know?

_____

_____

The caption for the second photograph tells us why this story is important for everybody. Why is it important?

_____

_____

Erik Weihenmayer achieved amazing things. How have his achievements inspired you? What is one thing you would like to do but think you cannot do? Draw an illustration of yourself doing this difficult thing. Write a caption that explains what you are doing.

_____

_____

_____

_____

Name _____ Date _____

Lesson 28
READER'S NOTEBOOK

Becoming Anything
He Wants to Be
Spelling: Words with
ough and *augh*

Words with *ough* and *augh*

Basic: Write the Basic Word that completes each sentence.

1. A mother and her _____ had a problem.

2. The little girl had _____ a bad cold.

3. Every day, the child's _____ grew worse.

4. Her sore throat made her voice _____ and scratchy.

5. The girl couldn't sleep _____ the night.

6. The mother knew she _____ to take the girl to a doctor.

7. They didn't have _____ money, though, to pay the bill.

8. Then the mother _____ of something.

9. Some of her neighbors had _____ to have a free clinic set up nearby.

10. She picked up her daughter and _____ her to the clinic.

Challenge: Write a sentence about a problem you had and how you solved it. Use both Challenge Words.

_____

_____

_____

Spelling Words

Basic
1. taught
2. thought
3. rough
4. laugh
5. bought
6. cough
7. ought
8. caught
9. fought
10. daughter
11. tough
12. through
13. enough
14. brought

Challenge
sought
naughty

Name _____ Date _____

Lesson 28
READER'S NOTEBOOK

Becoming Anything
He Wants to Be
Spelling: Words with
ough and *augh*

Word Sort

Write each Basic Word beside the correct heading.

Spelling Words

Basic
1. taught
2. thought
3. rough
4. laugh
5. bought
6. cough
7. ought
8. caught
9. fought
10. daughter
11. tough
12. through
13. enough
14. brought

Challenge
sought
naughty

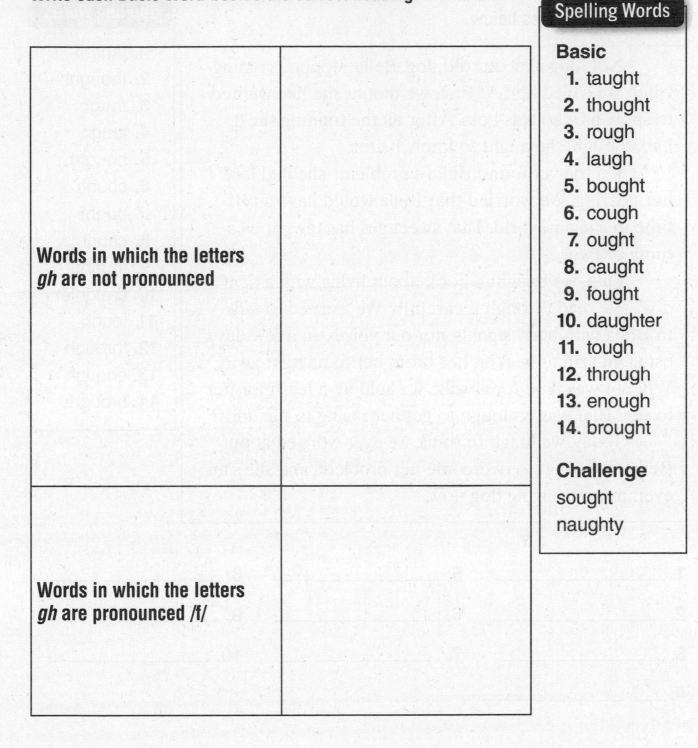

**Words in which the letters
gh are not pronounced**

**Words in which the letters
gh are pronounced /f/**

Challenge: Add the Challenge Words to your Word Sort.

Proofreading for Spelling

Find the misspelled words and circle them. Write them correctly on the lines below.

Not long ago, our old dog, Bella, stopped coming when we called her. At first, we thouht she just wanted to show us who was boss. After all the training she'd had, though, she aught to know better.

Then the vet found Bella's problem: she had lost her hearing. We worried that Bella would have a tuff time in a silent world. That sweet girl has tawght us a thing or two!

First, we baught a book about living with a deaf dog. We read throogh it carefully. We learned to talk to Bella with body signals, not our voices. In a few days, using an arm to beckon her brout her to us right away. When it was time for a walk, we held up a leash for her to see. That was ennough to get her racing to the door!

Today, we luagh to think we ever worried about Bella. She fougt to overcome her problem, and she's an even more amazing dog now.

Spelling Words

1. taught
2. thought
3. rough
4. laugh
5. bought
6. cough
7. ought
8. caught
9. fought
10. daughter
11. tough
12. through
13. enough
14. brought

1. _____   5. _____   8. _____

2. _____   6. _____   9. _____

3. _____   7. _____   10. _____

4. _____

Name _____ Date _____

Lesson 28
READER'S NOTEBOOK

Becoming Anything
He Wants to Be
Grammar: Commas in Sentences

Commas in a Series

- A **series** is a list of three or more words together in a sentence.
- Use a **comma** to separate the words in a series.

  It was <u>cold, wet, and windy</u> when he climbed the mountain.

Thinking Question
Is there a list of three or more words in the sentence?

Activity: Rewrite each sentence correctly. Add commas where they are needed.

1. He had a big breakfast of eggs toast and orange juice.

_____

_____

2. She packed up the tent backpack and sleeping bag.

_____

_____

3. The weather was cold windy and sunny.

_____

_____

4. They wore sunglasses hats and gloves.

_____

_____

5. Along the path they saw deer raccoons and a fox.

_____

_____

6. They would tell their story to Anna Julio and Wade.

_____

_____

189

Name _____ Date _____

Commas with Introductory Words

- Use a **comma** after the introductory words *well*, *yes*, and *no*.
- Use a comma after order words such as *first*, *second*, *next*, and *finally*.
- Do not use a comma after *then*.

  <u>Yes</u>, I might want to try climbing one day.

Thinking Question
Is there an introductory or order word in the sentence?

Rewrite these sentences correctly. Add commas where they are needed.

1. First let's have some lunch.

   _____

2. Yes that is a very good idea.

   _____

3. No I did not remember to fill the water bottles.

   _____

4. Well we will have to look for a water fountain.

   _____

5. Yes I can show you how to pack away the blanket.

   _____

6. First fold it neatly in half and then in half again.

   _____

7. Next smooth out any wrinkles.

   _____

8. Finally roll the blanket carefully, starting at one of the short ends.

   _____

Name _____ Date _____

Lesson 28
READER'S NOTEBOOK

Becoming Anything
He Wants to Be
Grammar: Commas in Sentences

Commas in Sentences

**Read each pair of sentences. Fill in the circle next to the
sentence that uses correct punctuation.**

1. Ⓐ Climbers can be tall, short, young, or old.

   Ⓑ Climbers can be tall short, young or, old.

2. Ⓐ Yes, climbing is one of my hobbies.

   Ⓑ Yes climbing is one of my hobbies.

3. Ⓐ Well reaching, a goal takes lots of hard work.

   Ⓑ Well, reaching a goal takes lots of hard work.

4. Ⓐ She used paper, markers, and scissors to draw her plan.

   Ⓑ She used paper, markers, and scissors, to draw her plan.

5. Ⓐ First, you have to decide if you are willing to do the work.

   Ⓑ First you have to decide if you are willing to do the work.

Writing Abbreviations

- An **abbreviation** is a short way to write a word. Most abbreviations begin with a capital letter and end with a period.

Abbreviations	
Sunday	Sun.
Monday	Mon.
September	Sept.
title for any woman	Ms.
title for married woman	Mrs.
street	St.
avenue	Ave.

1–10 Write each abbreviation correctly.

1. October _____

2. avenue _____

3. Tuesday _____

4. doctor Smith _____

5. Thursday _____

6. mister Hill _____

7. December _____

8. April _____

9. mister Adams _____

10. street _____

Sentence Fluency:
Combining Words to Form a Series

Choppy Sentences	Combined Nouns to Make a Series
He needs rope for climbing. He also needs gloves for climbing. He needs boots for climbing.	He needs rope, gloves, and boots for climbing.

Choppy Sentences	Combined Predicates to Make a Series
He wrestles. He scuba dives. He rides a bike.	He wrestles, scuba dives, and rides a bike.

Activity: Combine each group of sentences by forming a series of nouns, verbs, or phrases. Write the new sentence on the lines. Add commas where necessary.

1. Erik climbs walls. He climbs mountains. He also climbs

   hills.

   _____

   _____

2. Jose wants to share his success with his parents. He wants to share it with his friends. He wants to share his success with his neighbors.

   _____

   _____

3. Anika never gave up. She never complained. She never made excuses.

   _____

   _____

4. Fong practiced in the morning. He practiced at night. He practiced on the weekend. _____

   _____

Name _____ Date _____

Lesson 28
READER'S NOTEBOOK

Becoming Anything
He Wants to Be
Writing: Informative Writing

Focus Trait: Conventions

Read each step of the instructions for starting a rock collection. Rewrite the step with exact words and details to give more information.

1. Step: Get a box.

With Exact Words and Details:

_____

2. Step: Dig up some rocks.

With Exact Words and Details:

_____

_____

3. Step: Clean the rocks.

With Exact Words and Details:

_____

_____

4. Step: Put them away.

With Exact Words and Details:

_____

5. Step: Read about the rocks.

With Exact Words and Details:

_____

_____

Name _____ Date _____

Lesson 29
READER'S NOTEBOOK

A New Team of Heroes
Phonics: Words Ending in
-er or -le

Words Ending in *-er* or *-le*

Read the words in the box. Then choose the word that best matches each clue.

Word Bank
apple   better   farmer   little   member
middle   rattle   struggle   summer   supper

1. a red fruit that is sweet to eat _____

2. someone who belongs to a group _____

3. a meal you eat late in the day _____

4. not big; small _____

5. a person who grows food crops _____

6. a toy that a baby shakes _____

7. in between the first and the last _____

8. the opposite of *worse* _____

9. the opposite of *winter* _____

10. a fight or something difficult _____

Reader's Guide

A New Team of Heroes

The Story of the Game

Choose a character to tell about the soccer game in his or her own words. First, review the play to remember important details.

Read pages 48–50. What can we tell about Carla so far?

_____

_____

What do we learn about Lauren?

_____

_____

How does Hiro feel about Carla?

_____

_____

How does Gayle feel about Carla?

_____

_____

Read pages 51–52. What can we tell about Manny?

_____

_____

Think about the characters in the play: Carla, Lauren, Hiro, Gayle, and Manny. Imagine that one of the soccer players is writing a narrative about the game from his or her point of view. Use the box below to write the story.

My Story by _____

_____

_____

_____

_____

_____

_____

_____

_____

_____

Words Ending with -er or -le

Basic: Write the Basic Word that answers each clue.

1. The goal of someone who is making funny faces at you is to make you do this. _____

2. If your aunt is married, her husband is this. _____

3. Your goal is to make this color when you mix red and blue. _____

4. An archer's goal is to hit this part of a target. _____

5. A goal you plan to reach tomorrow is one you'll reach at this time. _____

6. Eating one of these a day can help you reach your goal of keeping the doctor away. _____

7. If a rooftop is your goal, this tool can help you. _____

8. Cooking a turkey dinner is the goal of many people in this month. _____

9. People often have a goal of building a snowman during this season. _____

10. A common goal during this season is to stay cool. _____

Spelling Words
Basic
1. apple
2. river
3. little
4. October
5. ladder
6. summer
7. purple
8. later
9. November
10. giggle
11. uncle
12. winter
13. center
14. double
Challenge
whistle
character

Challenge: Write two sentences telling how someone might reach a goal. Use both Challenge Words.

_____

_____

Name _____ Date _____

Lesson 29
READER'S NOTEBOOK

A New Team of Heroes
Spelling: Words Ending with
-*er* or -*le*

Word Sort

Write each Basic Word next to the correct heading.

Words that name seasons	
Words that name months of the year	
Words that name objects you can pick up	
Other words	

Challenge: Add the Challenge Words to your Word Sort.

Spelling Words

Basic
1. apple
2. river
3. little
4. October
5. ladder
6. summer
7. purple
8. later
9. November
10. giggle
11. uncle
12. winter
13. center
14. double

Challenge
whistle
character

Proofreading for Spelling

Find the misspelled words and circle them. Write them correctly on the lines below.

Try Out for the Basketball Team

Welcome back to school! We hope your sumer vacation was super.

As you all know, winnter is the season for basketball. This year, tryouts for our team will be held the last Monday in Ocktober. Practices will begin early in Novembar. In January, we'll travel across the rivier to play our first game against the Dunkers.

We urge all interested students, new or old, big or littel, to try out for the basketball team. You won't have to make a basket from the senter of the court. You must, though, be willing to dubble your efforts when it's needed.

So if you'd like to see yourself in our team's purpul uniform, just try out. That way, you won't be sorry laiter that you didn't.

Spelling Words

1. apple
2. river
3. little
4. October
5. ladder
6. summer
7. purple
8. later
9. November
10. giggle
11. uncle
12. winter
13. center
14. double

1. _____ 5. _____ 8. _____

2. _____ 6. _____ 9. _____

3. _____ 7. _____ 10. _____

4. _____

Lesson 29
READER'S NOTEBOOK

**A New Team
of Heroes**

Grammar:
What Is a Preposition?

What Is a Preposition?

Common Prepositions						
about	around	beside	for	near	outside	under
above	at	by	from	of	over	until
across	before	down	in	off	past	up
after	behind	during	inside	on	through	with
along	below	except	into	out	to	without

Underline the preposition in each sentence.

1. Some people like to hike the trails around a lake.

2. Hiking over the hills is good exercise.

3. In summer, flowers cover the hills.

4. Some people like the mountains in winter.

5. They ski or snowboard down the steep slopes.

6. A high mountain is a challenge for climbers.

7. Reaching the top of a mountain is a climber's goal.

8. Climbers usually hike with a guide.

9. Guides know the safest way to the top.

10. Which mountains in our country do you know about?

Name _____ Date _____

Lesson 29
READER'S NOTEBOOK

A New Team of Heroes
Grammar:
What Is a Preposition?

Prepositional Phrases

1–5. Underline the prepositional phrase in each sentence.

1. Those people in the distance are taking a hike.

2. I wonder how far they will hike before lunch?

3. We can follow the hikers up the hill.

4. My friend from the city likes hiking, too.

5. Let's hike to that tall pine tree.

6–10. Underline two prepositional phrases in each sentence. Write the prepositional phrase that tells *when*.

6. On Friday, our class took a hike in the woods.

_____

7. I didn't think we were going on the hike until next week.

_____

8. We rested beside a creek at noon.

_____

9. During our rest, we looked at a distant mountain.

_____

10. By the afternoon, we were all very tired from the long hike.

_____

Name _____ Date _____

Lesson 29
READER'S NOTEBOOK

**A New Team
of Heroes**
Grammar:
What Is a Preposition?

Prepositional Phrases

1–5. Underline the prepositional phrase in each sentence.

1. We use mountains for many things.

2. Rock climbers like to climb up mountain cliffs.

3. Miners search the rock for metals.

4. Trees growing on mountains supply logs for houses.

5. Cows and sheep can graze around a mountain's base.

6–10. Underline the prepositional phrases in each sentence. Write the prepositional phrase that tells *where*.

6. The weather on a mountain can change in a few minutes.

_____

7. It is very cold at the top of a mountain.

_____

8. At great heights, there is little oxygen for breathing.

_____

9. Many of the world's highest mountains are in Asia.

_____

10. Very few people live on these high mountains.

_____

Name _____ Date _____

Lesson 29
READER'S NOTEBOOK

Kinds of Adverbs

A New Team of Heroes
Grammar: Spiral Review

- An **adverb** is a word that describes a verb.
- **Adverbs** can come before or after the verb they are describing.
- Adverbs tell *how, when,* and *where* an action happens.

Adverb That Tells How	Adverb That Tells When	Adverb That Tells Where
Manny **quickly** passed the ball.	We have to practice **often.**	We practice **here** at the park.

1–4. Write the adverb and what it tells about each underlined verb.

1. Gayle <u>cheered</u> loudly for Manny. _____

2. They <u>ran</u> away from the fire. _____

3. The game always <u>begins</u> at 4:00. _____

4. Our team <u>shook</u> hands happily with the other team.

_____

5–8. Rewrite the sentences below into one sentence.

5. The team played another game. They played the game later.

_____

6. The goalie blocked the ball. He did it easily.

_____

7. We stop for water breaks. We stop often.

_____

8. Manny scores a goal. He always scores a goal.

_____

Sentence Fluency

Short, choppy sentences can be combined to make
your writing smoother. You can combine two sentences
by **moving a prepositional phrase**.

Two Sentences	Combined Sentence
We watched the film about mountains. We watched the film on Tuesday.	We watched the film about mountains on Tuesday.

**Combine two short choppy sentences by moving a prepositional phrase
to combine two sentences. Write the new sentence on the line.**

1. The map is on the wall.

The map is behind Mrs. Brown's desk.

_____

2. We can see the mountains in Asia.

We can see the mountains on the map.

_____

3. Please show me the mountains of Africa.

Please show me the mountains on the map.

_____

4. We will learn more about mountains.

We will learn more after lunch.

_____

5. Have you ever hiked in the mountains?

Have you ever hiked in our state?

_____

Focus Trait: Evidence

Read each pair of sentences. Underline the fact. Draw a line through the opinion. Then write a fact to replace the opinion.

1. In football, a touchdown scores 6 points. It is easy to score points.

Fact: _____

2. Golf is the hardest sport. Golfers use clubs to hit the ball.

Fact: _____

3. Swimmers should wear red suits. Many swimmers begin at a young age.

Fact: _____

4. A baseball catcher wears a mask. Everyone should have a turn to catch.

Fact: _____

5. All schools should have sports teams. Many children play sports.

Fact: _____

Sort the Words

Read each word in the box. Find the vowel that makes the schwa sound. Then write the word in the chart under the spelling of the schwa sound.

Word Bank					
about	actor	alive	cactus	camel	circus
engine	kennel	pencil	pilot	salad	wagon

schwa spelled *a*	schwa spelled *e*	schwa spelled *i*

schwa spelled *o*	schwa spelled *u*	

Reader's Guide

Saving Buster

Pet Reporter

You are a reporter. You are going to write a newspaper article about Buster's accident and how the neighbors helped. Newspaper reporters ask questions to find facts for their stories. Use the questions below to find facts. Then write the newspaper article.

Read pages 66–67. What happened to Buster?

_____

_____

Read page 68. What is the problem that Donovan wants to help solve?

_____

_____

Read pages 70–71. What was Donovan's idea for solving the problem?

_____

_____

Read pages 72–73. Did Donovan's solution raise the $2,000 needed to pay for Buster's care?

_____

_____

Now you know the facts about Buster's accident and how the neighborhood helped solve the problem.
It is time to write your article for the local paper.
Remember to include a headline or title for your story and an illustration.

Words that Begin with *a* or *be*

Basic: Write the Basic Word that completes each sentence.

Spelling Words

Basic
1. below
2. about
3. belong
4. around
5. again
6. alone
7. because
8. above
9. between
10. alive
11. behind
12. begin
13. along
14. before

Challenge
awhile
beyond

1. I was walking _____ my street when I spotted a kitten.

2. When it ran _____ my legs, I fell over!

3. Dad guessed the kitten is _____ two months old.

4. Dad said I could bring the kitten inside _____ it was cold out.

5. Then the kitten hid in a dark place _____ the couch.

6. _____ I could get it out, I had to move furniture.

7. The kitten jumped up on a shelf _____ the fireplace.

8. It followed a toy _____ in a circle.

9. The kitten made me laugh over and over _____ .

10. Dad and I agree that the kitten and I _____ together.

Challenge 11–12: Write two sentences about animals. Use both Challenge Words.

_____

_____

Word Sort

Write each Basic Word next to the correct heading.

Second syllable has three letters	
Second syllable has four letters	
Second syllable has five letters	

Challenge: Add the Challenge Words to your Word Sort.

Spelling Words

Basic
1. below
2. about
3. belong
4. around
5. again
6. alone
7. because
8. above
9. between
10. alive
11. behind
12. begin
13. along
14. before

Challenge
awhile
beyond

Proofreading for Spelling

Saving Buster
Spelling: Words that Begin with
a or *be*

Find the misspelled words and circle them. Write them correctly on the lines below.

Monday, July 9

 This past weekend, our family took part in a barn raising. I'd never heard abowt these events befoar. In a barn raising, a lot of people who bilong to a community get together to build a barn. No community member has to face the huge job of building a barn aloan.

 At first, I just walked arround the barnyard. I didn't know where to bigin to help. Soon, a man called from a beam abuve me. "Son, could you please bring me some nails?" he asked. I leaped into action becauze I wanted to be part of the group. I set up a ladder balow the man and handed him the nails.

 After that I worked hard all weekend, and that barn is done. It's a beauty! I would sure love to be part of a barn raising agenn.

Spelling Words

1. below
2. about
3. belong
4. around
5. again
6. alone
7. because
8. above
9. between
10. alive
11. behind
12. begin
13. along
14. before

1. _____ 5. _____ 8. _____

2. _____ 6. _____ 9. _____

3. _____ 7. _____ 10. _____

4. _____

Using *I* and *Me*

- Use the pronoun *I* only as the subject of a sentence. Always capitalize the word *I*.

    I am going to school.

- Use the pronoun *me* only as an object pronoun. When you talk about another person and yourself, it is polite to list yourself last.

    Julie handed the books to Lucy and **me**.

Thinking Question
Is the pronoun the subject or the object of the sentence?

Activity: Write the pronoun *I* or *me* to complete each sentence.

1. _____ watched my dog chase the ball.

2. Dad and _____ entered a dish in the potluck contest.

3. Amy went to the vet with my dog Sparky and _____.

4. My service dog helps _____ cross the street.

5. Can _____ help you plan the contest?

6. _____ liked the pasta salad the best.

7. The judge couldn't decide, so she gave the first prize to both Andy and _____.

8. _____ own a black dog named Ruby.

9. Ruby has been with my sister and _____ since I was five years old.

10. Someday _____ would like to train puppies to be service dogs.

Pronouns and Homophones

Homophones are words that sound alike but have different spellings and different meanings. Be sure to choose the correct homophone. Using the wrong homophone changes the meaning of the sentence.

Thinking Question
What are the clues in the sentence?

Homophone	Meaning	Example
its	belonging to it	The dog wagged **its** tail.
it's	it is	**It's** very cold outside.
your	belonging to you	I like **your** watch.
you're	you are	**You're** going to be late!
there	at or in that place	The book is over **there**.
their	belonging to them	**Their** dog can do tricks.
they're	they are	**They're** going to the store.

Activity: Read the sentences. Circle the correct homophones.

1. Dog training can be a fun activity for both you and **your you're** dog.

2. **Its It's** important to work with your dog every day.

3. Dogs perform best when **their they're** praised for good behavior.

4. If **your you're** patient with your dog, you can teach him or her to roll over.

5. **It's Its** important to train a puppy.

6. You can buy a leash at a pet supply store. Ask a clerk to help you when you get **there they're.**

7. The best time to train **your you're** dog is when he or she is young.

8. Dogs can still be trained when **there they're** older, too.

Correct Pronouns

Read each pair of sentences. Fill in the circle next to the sentence that uses the correct pronoun.

1. Ⓐ Mom and I will make dinner.

   Ⓑ Mom and me will make dinner.

2. Ⓐ The dog brought the ball to Marisa and I.

   Ⓑ The dog brought the ball to Marisa and me.

3. Ⓐ They're dog was trained to be a service dog.

   Ⓑ Their dog was trained to be a service dog.

4. Ⓐ It's fun to teach a dog to do tricks.

   Ⓑ Its fun to teach a dog to do tricks.

5. Ⓐ I saw your mom at the store.

   Ⓑ I saw you're mom at the store.

Making Comparisons

- **Adjectives** describe nouns. They can also show how people, places, and things are alike and different.

Comparing with Adjectives		
compare two	add -*er*	taller
compare three or more	add -*est*	tallest

- **Adverbs** describe verbs. For adverbs that end in -*ly*, add **more** to compare two actions. Add **most** to compare three or more actions.

1–4. **Write the correct form of the adjective in parentheses to complete each sentence.**

1. Molly was the _____ of all the service dogs. (small)

2. The Smiths were _____ than our other neighbors were. (friendly)

3. Of all of her classmates, Liz's voice is the _____. (strong)

4. Doug was the _____ member of the class. (young)

5–6. **Rewrite the sentences, combining each pair of sentences.**

5. Ralph is smarter than the cat. He is quicker too. _____

_____

6. Of all the dogs in the park, Benny has the biggest feet.
   He also has the longest tail. _____

_____

Name _____ Date _____

Conventions

Sentence with incorrect use of *I* and *me*	Corrected sentence
Me and my mom did everything we could to help out.	<u>My mom and I</u> did everything we could to help out.

Sentence with incorrect homophone	Corrected sentence
Their cooking wonderful food for the dinner tonight.	<u>They're</u> cooking wonderful food for the dinner tonight.

Proofread each sentence. Check for the correct use of the pronouns *I* and *me* and the correct use of homophones. Write the corrected sentence on the line.

1. David and me think the cooking contest will be fun.

   _____

2. They gave they're food to me and my mom.

   _____

3. The dog left the bone over their.

   _____

4. Its amazing how much money was raised.

   _____

5. Me and my friends think it's important to help you're neighbors.

   _____

6. Its good when people help each other.

   _____

7. You can help them by watching there dog.

   _____

8. They're dog loves to play.

Focus Trait: Organization

**Read each paragraph. Cross out the detail that does not tell about the main idea.
Then add a fact or a detail sentence that supports the main idea.**

1. Other animals pull vehicles. Oxen pulled pioneers' wagons
   in the 1800s. Locomotive trains can pull many cars. Some
   kinds of horses pull sleighs and carriages.

   _____

   _____

2. Several types of animals carry people. For hundreds of years,
   people have ridden horses. Donkeys can carry people through
   rough terrain. Lots of kids ride bicycles to school. Some people
   also ride camels.

   _____

   _____

3. In a beehive, different bees have different jobs. The queen lays
   eggs. Worker bees do a few jobs. They help make wax. They
   also feed other bees and help protect the hive. Some people
   are allergic to bees.

   _____

   _____

4. Dogs do different kinds of work. Chihuahuas are a tiny kind of
   dog. There are herding dogs and police dogs. Some dogs are
   even actors!

   _____

   _____

Reading and Writing Glossary

Use this glossary to help you remember and use words that you are learning about reading and writing.

A

abstract noun A noun that names an idea, a feeling, or a quality. Abstract nouns are things that people cannot see, hear, taste, smell, or touch.

action verb A verb that tells what people or things do.

adjective A word that describes a noun. Adjectives may also be used to compare nouns.

adverb A word that describes a verb, adjective, or other adverb. Adverbs may tell how, when, or where an action takes place.

analogy A kind of comparison in which one pair of words is compared to another. Each pair relates by definition, meaning, or characteristics.

analyze To look at or study carefully.

antecedent The noun that a pronoun replaces.

antonym A word that has the opposite, or nearly the opposite, meaning than another word.

article A word, such as *a, an,* or *the,* that comes before a noun. Articles tell which noun.

author's purpose The reason an author has for writing.

B

base word A word to which endings, prefixes, and suffixes can be added.

biography A story about the events in a person's life told in time order.

C

....

caption Text that explains a photo or picture.

cause An event that makes something else happen.

character A person in a story.

chart A drawing that lists information in a way that makes it clear and easy to understand.

clarify To make clear.

comma Punctuation mark that tells a reader where to pause. A comma can also help to make a sentence's meaning more clear.

command A type of sentence that gives an order. A command may end with a period (.) or an exclamation mark (!).

common noun A noun that names any person, place, or thing.

compare To decide how people and things are alike.

complex sentence A sentence with two parts, a simple sentence and a dependent clause.

compound sentence A sentence made up of two simple sentences joined by a conjunction.

conclusion A good guess about something the author does not say directly.

conjunction Joining words such as *and, or, but,* and *so.* Conjunctions appear after a comma in a compound sentence.

context Sentences or details that help explain a particular word or phrase.

contrast To decide how people and things are different.

D

....

dependent clause A group of words that does not express a complete thought. A dependent clause may be found in a complex sentence.

detail Facts and examples that give more information about the main idea.

diagram An illustration that shows important details, such as how something works. A diagram may have labels or captions to tell what its parts show.

dictionary A reference book that contains an alphabetical list of words along with their meanings, pronunciations, parts of speech, and other information.

dictionary entry A word and its definition listed in a dictionary or glossary.

digital dictionary A reference source available online or on portable disks that provides meanings for words.

directions Text that tells how to do something step by step.

domain The subject a text is about.

domain-specific vocabulary Words related to a specific topic, such as science.

drama A story written to be acted out.

E

....

effect An event that happens because of an earlier action.

evaluate To form an opinion about something.

exclamation A sentence that shows a strong feeling and ends with an exclamation point (!).

expository nonfiction Text that gives facts about what something is, how something works, or why something is important.

F

fable A short story in which a character, usually an animal that behaves like a person, learns a lesson.

fact Something that can be proved true.

fairy tale A kind of traditional tale with magical characters and events.

fantasy An imaginative story with characters or events that are not real.

feelings A person's emotions about something or someone.

folktale A story that has been told for many years. A folktale often has a moral, or lesson.

formal language A serious and polite form of speaking or writing.

future tense Verb form which describes a future action.

G

glossary A text feature found at the end of a book that provides an alphabetical listing of specialized words, their meanings, and other information.

graphic features Artwork, such as pictures, diagrams, and charts, that gives readers more information about the text.

H

heading Tells the reader what a section of text is about.

historical fiction A story that is set in the past and tells about things that could happen in a real time and place.

homograph A word that has the same spelling as another word but has a different meaning and may be pronounced differently.

homophone A word that sounds the same as another word but is spelled differently and has a different meaning.

humorous fiction Story that has characters and events that are funny. The setting and characters may be unrealistic.

I

idiom An expression with a special meaning different from the usual meanings of the individual words.

illustration Artwork that helps show a story's events.

imagery The use of vivid descriptions that help readers form an image, or picture, in their minds.

informal language A more relaxed form of speaking or writing.

informational text Text that gives factual information about a topic.

informative writing Writing that gives facts about a topic.

L

legend An old story that people have told for many years. The events of the story may or may not be true.

literal meaning The exact meaning of a word or phrase.

M

main idea The most important idea in a text.

map A drawing of an area, such as a neighborhood, town, or state.

message A story's lesson or moral.

monitor To check one's understanding.

mood The overall feeling of a story.

moral A lesson that is usually taught through something that happens to a main character or through what the character learns.

motivation The reason a character acts a certain way.

myth A story that tells what a group of people believe about the world.

N

narrative nonfiction A selection that gives information about a topic but is told as a story.

narrative writing Writing that tells a story. A narrative tells about something that happened to a person or a character.

nonliteral meaning The symbolic or figurative meaning of a word.

noun Names a person, a place, or a thing.

O

object pronoun A word that takes the place of the object: *me, you, him, her, it, us, them*. An object pronoun follows action verbs and words such as *to, for, at, of,* and *with*.

opinion Something that tells someone's thought, feeling, or belief.

opinion writing Writing that tells what the writer believes and gives reasons.

P

part of speech The way a word is used in a sentence, for example, noun, verb, or adjective.

past tense Verb form which describes a past action.

photograph Shows true pictures of important text details.

play A story that can be performed for an audience.

plot The problem that characters face and the events of the story.

plural noun A noun that names more than one person, place, or thing.

poetry Uses the sound and rhythm of words to show images and express feelings.

point of view How one thinks or feels about a subject.

possessive noun Shows that a person or animal owns or has something.

possessive pronoun Takes the place of a possessive noun to show who or what owns or has something.

precise words Words that are descriptive and exact.

predicate The action part of the sentence that tells what the subject does or did.

prefix A word part added to the beginning of a base word. A prefix changes the meaning of the base word but cannot stand alone.

present tense Verb form which describes action that happens in the present.

pronoun A word that takes the place of one or more nouns in a sentence.

proper noun A noun that names a particular person, place, or thing. A proper noun begins with a capital letter.

Q

question A type of sentence that asks something and ends with a question mark (?).

question To ask yourself questions about a selection before, during, and after reading.

quotation marks Punctuation marks (" ") that indicate dialogue. Quotation marks show the exact words a person says.

R

realistic fiction Story that has characters and events that are like those in real life.

research report Writing that tells what a writer learned from doing research about a topic.

rhyme When words end with the same sound. Rhyme is often found in poems.

run-on An error in which a writer joins two simple sentence without using a comma or a conjunction.

S

scene A section division of a play, similar to chapters in a book.

sequence The order in which different steps or events happen.

series When you list three or more words together in a sentence. Commas separate the words in a series.

series books Books that tell different stories about the same character.

setting Where and when a story takes place.

shades of meaning Slight differences in meaning among words that are related, especially words that describe degrees of certainty.

signal word A word that indicates a cause and its effect.

simple sentence A group of words that tells a complete thought. A simple sentence has a subject and a predicate.

singular noun A noun that names only one person, place, or thing.

stage directions Instructions to actors on how to move and speak.

stanza A group of lines in a poem. Stanzas often follow a rhyming pattern.

statement A type of sentence that tells something and ends with a period (.).

steps in a procedure Directions that are written in sequence.

story structure The characters, setting, and plot of a story.

subject The naming part of a sentence that tells *who* or *what*.

subject pronoun A word that takes the place of a subject: *I, you, he, she, it, we, they*.

subordinating conjunction Joins a dependent clause to the main part of a sentence. Some subordinating conjunctions are *because, after, when,* and *if.*

suffix A word part that is added to the end of a base word. A suffix changes the meaning of the base word but cannot stand alone.

summarize To briefly tell the important parts of a text in your own words.

synonym A word that has the same, or nearly the same, meaning as another word.

T

text and graphic features Sidebars, diagrams, and photographs outside of the main body of the text.

text features Parts of text, such as special type, speech balloons, and labels, that help readers find information.

theme An author's message about life to the reader.

thesaurus A book that provides a list of words, arranged in alphabetical order, and their synonyms.

timeline A line that shows the order in which events happened.

traditional tale A story that people have told for many years.

traits A person's qualities.

trickster tale An imaginative story in which one character tricks another.

V

verb The main word in the predicate.

visualize To create a mental picture.

W

word ending A word part, such as -s, -ed, or -er, added to the end of a base word.

word family A group of words with a common pattern, such as the same base word.

word root A word part from which other words are formed.